The Smoke Charmer's Tale

Rosannah Killian

Reformation
Lightning

Reformation Lightning

British Library Cataloguing in Publication Data
A record for this book is available from the British Library

ISBN: 978-1-916669-01-7

Cover design by Chris Iliff (ChrisIliff.co.uk)
Additional design by Pete Barnsley (CreativeHoot.com)

Printed in Great Britain

Reformation Lightning, an imprint of 10Publishing
Unit C, Tomlinson Road, Leyland, PR25 2DY, England

1 3 5 7 10 8 6 4 2

1

A Small Step

Ada looked around wildly as she was pulled along. The underground river gurgled expectantly from unseen depths below. One push and she would be washed away.

O Mother Levia please, no!

Ada thrashed and writhed. She screeched. Her captor paused to shift his grip on her: a giant arm squeezed tighter around her chest and the fleshy hand blocking her mouth shifted to pinch her nose shut. Her lungs heaved but no air came. Her throat began to burn. In panicking strength, she threw her body this way and that. Her feet kicked the air, bounced against his legs, then found the wall. She pushed off the stones hard.

The man staggered but caught himself. He shook her and a voice rasped into her ear, "Careful or you'll have us both in."

Pulling her closer into his crushing grip, he plodded along the walkway, onwards into the dark, dogged by the rushing voice of the invisible torrent.

I'm going to die down here. I'm going to die. But it's too soon – too soon!

They turned into a large chamber, where a pale gleam of distant daylight was barred by rows of thick columns. Light meant a way to the surface. Ada struggled afresh but could only jerk feebly.

A shadow detached itself from one of the columns. Voices spoke but they were lost in the rushing throb of her ears and the all-consuming burning spreading down inside her chest.

Air...air...she needed...

The giant released her. Ada sank to the ground gasping, her senses reeling.

Before she could get her bearings, something rocketed past her and the giant crashed down with an angry yell. A fresh pair of hands scooped Ada up and tossed her sideways, sending her flying like a rag doll. She hit the ground heavily, driving out that precious first lungful of air.

Behind her an ear-splitting yowl echoed and re-echoed against stone. The air wrestled with fury and sound.

Gulping breaths, Ada scrambled onto all fours and crawled further into the thick darkness, trying to get away.

The ground ahead vanished: her arm and wrist jarred against the stone edge of the drop. Her fingertips caught rising spray. A new roaring rushed up from below. She had found the water channel. If she fell down there, she would be sucked underground to drown. Ada backed away, tried a different direction and hit a wall.

"Get out of 'ere," snarled a voice.

Ada looked back. Against the pale stretch of light, she saw the two silhouetted figures of her attackers running away. The victor stood, motionless as the pillars, watching them long after the sounds of their retreat had faded.

He turned his whole body towards her.

Ada stiffened.

"Are you all right?"

She didn't answer, she couldn't. Her voice was frozen, locked inside.

The stranger leapt into her darkened patch. She flinched backwards into the wall.

There was a sharp scraping, a flurry of sparks, a flicker of light and a flame spurted into life. The stranger held it up close to her face. She squinted in the sudden dazzle and cocked her head away from the brightness to get a better look at him. He followed the motion with his hand, blocking her line of sight with the flame.

"You're not hurt – not seriously." The voice was level, almost bored. "Don't move. Wait for them to find you." He tossed the burning wick away. She caught a passing glimpse of his face: not young, but not old; his glass skin was nearly as smooth as hers, catching the flamelight and refracting it into faint ripples of colour. He was gone.

It was dark.

"No, wait!"

Ada stumbled upright and stopped. Everything immediately around her was in utter blackness: a great slab of rock blocked the hint of daylight from reaching anything near her feet. Ada inched forwards cautiously. Her foot felt the edge of a step – or was it a drop? She tentatively reached down but felt only air. If there was a step it had been intended for someone with unnaturally long legs. She stared hard, willing herself to see. Her eyes ached with the effort but she remained as blind as before. She continued feeling the ground until she was reluctantly convinced that she was on a square island cut off by water channels and a wall. Her rescuer must have known this chamber inside out to throw her here, never mind crossing the channels twice in the dark.

Cold air rushed through the tunnel, merging with the sound of the churning water. A drip plopped methodically. No other noise broke the silence.

She stood irresolute, feeling appallingly helpless. No, it wasn't merely a feeling, she *was* appallingly helpless. Both her kidnappers and her rescuer were evidently masters of navigating these dark regions; she was useless. She wondered about her rescuer again. He hadn't been overly helpful, abandoning her. He hadn't even left her with the light, but had instead casually tossed it away into the water.

"Don't move. Wait for them to find you," Ada muttered in mimicry. As if she had a choice, with the death trap of water channels surrounding her. Or perhaps that was his intention, that she should be trapped here, ready and waiting to be collected by slavers or...or...

"Lady Ada?" The voice was stretched thin by distance but recognisable.

"Meruda!" Ada cried, unable to mask the relief in her voice. "I'm here."

Meruda began to bless every known dragon but was overridden by a deeper voice: "Don't move, my lady! Just keep still and keep calling and we'll come to you."

As Ada continued calling and Meruda's replies grew more distinct, a faint glow crept along the walls until it burst around the corner with painful brightness. Ada quickly shielded her eyes and turned to examine her now visible surroundings. Her deductions had been largely correct: although she was backed against one of the columns and not a wall, she was boxed in by deep water channels. Those channels, while certainly wide enough to fall into (Ada was glad she had not attempted anything in the dark) were narrow enough to be covered by a short jump. Feeling some energy return, she gathered up her skirts and leapt neatly over.

Meruda shrieked in alarm and ran up scolding, only to laugh and cry and begin to check Ada over for any injury. The people with her – Ada recognised her coachman, while the rest wore the uniform of the Watch – raised their lanterns high to help her. They were gloomy lights, casting everything in a greenish grey, or was it that everything down here was a greenish grey, even Meruda's face? Her maid's naturally rosy countenance was blanched. The effect was increased by the light from a lantern streaming sideways through her outer glass skin, which made half her face luminescent. If not for her physical touch, she could have passed for the phantom at the gates of death.

Ada quickly brushed Meruda aside. Relief was threatening to turn her legs to jelly. Best keep going. She smiled at the attending crowd.

"Thank you everybody for coming to look for me," she said with gracious condescension. She had long ago learnt that her voice was less likely to wobble when speaking with gracious condescension. "I am so sorry to have put you to so much trouble – thank you Meruda, that will do. Now, I assume we don't intend to remain here all day?"

"Sorry, my lady," said the coachman, stepping aside. "This way my lady."

"Yes, come on dear," Meruda said, attempting to wrap her arm around Ada's shoulders.

Ada shook her off and turned to the leader of the Watch. "Are you familiar with these tunnels?"

He deferred the answer to another man, who apparently knew these passages like the back of his mother's hand. As he clearly meant that to be a reassuring statement, Ada enquired if there were other exits to the surface.

"There'd be half a dozen of those, ma'am."

Ada allowed herself an indulgent smile at the misuse of the title. Ma'am indeed! The man probably had no idea of the correct terms of address for the nobility, or perhaps he didn't know exactly who she was. That would be almost too good to be true.

"Very well then, choose one that comes out onto a quiet thoroughfare. Then one of you go with my coachman and bring the carriage around to meet us there. I prefer not to be a spectacle for the marketeers."

"Of course, ma'am."

Everything worked beautifully, better than Ada thought possible. The few minutes blurred by: walking through the dark passages; up the steps into beautiful fresh air; waiting in an alcove in the miraculously quiet street; the carriage rumbling towards them; quickly climbing up and in; throwing a purse of coins at the Watch with a last word of thanks and trundling homewards.

Ada pulled the curtains shut over the carriage windows and flopped back, sagging into the cushions, trembling.

Meruda copied her example by closing the other window, then leant forward and began trying to remove the grimy marks left on Ada's dress. Ada let her get on with it, staring into the curtain. She tried to reel her thoughts in, but they would keep running and rerunning over the events in the tunnels, growing ever more frightened and confused.

"A *paddle is meant to paddle, not fill your boat with water*."

Startled, Ada looked up.

Meruda grasped her hands.

"Look at me, my lady. Breathe. That's it: deep breaths... slowly...good. You are drowning in your own thoughts. When you are ready, speak and direct them; don't let them overwhelm you."

Ada inhaled deeply. Her shoulders slowly dropped. Her thoughts calmed. Yet she resented needing the help: she was a Dura!

"Do you always have to quote Vlainshai?"

"You needed distracting and the proverb seemed appropriate," Meruda replied, unruffled. "Would something ridiculous have been better? Dolphins dancing down the street?"

Ada half-choked on a laugh but it warped into a sob.

"That's better: let it out. You've had a shock."

Ada yanked a hand free to brush her cheeks dry. If she were going to talk, she would be cool and collected. She built an imaginary wall to block out the feelings, breathed slowly, and waited until she was confident that her voice wouldn't wobble.

"I feel such a fool for letting it happen and I'm terrified my father will find out."

"Why? He's your father, one of the most powerful men in Aven. If you describe what your attacker was like and –"

"There were two of them," Ada interrupted. "One was a giant of a man, but I didn't see either of them clearly; I was seized from behind and it was dark when the other man scared them off."

"Other man?" Meruda echoed. "But you were alone when we arrived."

"He left before you came."

"Well, perhaps we can track him down: Lord Dura will want to reward him."

"I don't want father to know anything about it. My father..." Ada trailed off, unwilling to explain. In the six months that Meruda had served her, Lord Dura had scarcely visited. Even now that he had summoned Ada from their southern home to the capital city, Casida, she had only seen him twice. How could Meruda know what he was like? But Ada knew how he would react if he heard about today's little excitement: a scathing lecture, guards set to watch her every move and Meruda would probably be blamed and dismissed.

"But surely we ought to find the culprits?" Meruda persisted.

Ada laughed bitterly. "Assassins aren't usually easy to find."

"Assassins!" Meruda snorted. "They were far too sloppy, and why drag you away captive? It's more likely they were common scoundrels who took a chance. Did they take anything?"

"Only that ugly purse Lady Humber gave me, which was empty anyway. If they had simply robbed me of that I should have thanked them."

"There you are then: clumsy thieves. And provided you don't go wandering off like that again you needn't worry about them. Thank the dragons that child spotted you being taken and the Watch were so nearby, not to mention your mysterious rescuer. Perhaps he's a secret admirer?"

Ada rolled her eyes, happy to play along with the teasing.

Meruda began unfastening the curtain tassels. "Now after all that, I think you could do with some fresh air and talking about happier things." Her cheerful chatter ran on unabated. Ada enjoyed the sound without listening as she looked out of the window.

There were too many unanswered questions for her to feel truly calm, questions not only about her kidnappers but her rescuer: his identity, his sudden appearance and the haunting familiarity of the face she had glimpsed. Was that imagination or had she seen him somewhere before? Vague suspicions gnawed at her gut.

Ada shook herself. She couldn't think clearly now: she would only make herself sick with worry and wouldn't solve anything. Best come back to it with a clear head. Pushing away the circling doubts, she concentrated on the passing sights instead. The distraction was successful.

She watched the passing city of Casida mesmerised, dizzy with seeing so much so quickly. Winding streets opened out into large paved squares, invariably centred around a water feature; market stalls were crammed into every conceivable space; people rushed, shouted, babbled; the dome of the dragnoss loomed –

The carriage turned sharply. With a jolt, Ada realised that they had already reached her father's mansion and were entering the gates.

She was relieved to see that her father wasn't waiting for her on the threshold, but if he was mercifully absent, nobody else was. The house was a hive of organised chaos. Servants were feverishly polishing every solid thing in sight, tapestries were being examined, floors scrubbed and boxes were being carried here and there.

Ada frowned as she picked her way through the entrance hall. Someone ought to have at least formally acknowledged her return.

"Lady Ada," the household chamberlain hurried up, bowing as he came.

About time too. Ada stood still, chin raised, and waited for him to come to her.

He halted in front of her and offered her a letter. "Your father left this for you and the seamstress will be with you within the hour."

Why should her father be sending her a seamstress? She had enough dresses. Ada broke the wax seal, read and understood. The paper trembled. Ada refolded the letter with deliberate care. The paper stilled.

"Meruda, go to my chambers and ensure all is ready for the seamstress."

"Very good, my lady."

Ada turned to the chamberlain. "Where is Master Kessler?"

His lip curled an unforgivable fraction. "The high steward is on the lower terrace. He asked that no-one disturb him."

"Good. See that no-one does." She stalked down the hallway towards the garden, clutching the letter. After all the years of waiting, this was why her father had finally summoned her to Casida. She should have known it would be something like this. What would her dear old Kessler say?

She found Kessler pacing below a tall hedge, out of sight from the house, not that she trusted anything in a city to be truly private.

Kessler halted at her approach, hands clasped behind his back, his eyes grave under a careworn forehead. He appeared to have aged since she had gone out this morning, his locks more grizzled and his habitual stoop exaggerated as if he were carrying a heavy weight. His eyes met hers. He knew. In that instant she realised that he had always known why they had been summoned.

And he had never told her.

Silence.

"I believe you are meant to congratulate me," she finally said. His eyes flickered to the letter.

He stirred, slowly drawing himself up to his proper height, a kind, sad smile on his face.

"Yes, yes...I wish you all felicity on your engagement, my lady."

She glanced once more up at the house and the garden, before sitting down on a bench. The flat stone had been in the shade all afternoon; the cold quickly penetrated her dress. She looked down at her lap. Despite Meruda's best efforts, she saw traces of the tunnel grime. She was back there now, back in the dark, struggling to breathe, struggling for freedom, only instead of a giant, a seamstress was coming to entrap her, not by a strangulating hold but in a dress for a betrothal ceremony.

And Kessler had known and not told her. The betrayal numbed her. She longed to confide in him as she always had, but hurt paralysed her voice to a stone.

In the past when she was upset, Kessler would have sat beside her and said something comforting, just one kind word at which her thoughts, fears and pent-up emotions would come flooding out. He would have listened patiently for however long she needed, before soothing and calming her with some wise and tested truth. That was what he had done for as long as she could remember. If only he would act normally now and help her to confide in him again. But he did not. Instead, he remained rooted in the same spot, keeping a respectful distance. This was the new life, was it?

"I expect you have duties to attend to," she eventually said.

He murmured assent and took his leave.

Ada stared past him into empty space and continued to stare. It was several minutes before she realised that she was crying.

2

Emergence

"*We are the race of lantyn.*"

Ada il Dura shivered. Candlelight bounced off her glass skin at the movement. Tiny gems of light and rainbow filaments danced over the walls. How many people were out there, waiting for her behind the doors?

The ocean of voices rumbled relentlessly through the wood:

" – *We serve the dragons' lore.*

Our hearts are dark without their light;
The Grey Realm endless night.
Come to us, our hearts' desire:
Claim us. Possess us. Burn us with your fire!"

Ada's stomach churned. Did the Dragons' Creed really say that? Yes of course it did, she knew it did: she had been taught to recite it as soon as she could talk. Yet listening to the words felt different to saying them. Or perhaps it was simply the volume that was alarming: it sounded as if her father had gathered the entire court.

Did she have to go through with this? Strange to ask that when she had looked forward to this day for so long; betrothal opened up the way to finally being someone with recognition at court and the power to do something. Yet the shadowy far-off prospect had never been this nerve-wracking.

The sound outside shifted into a new rhythm.

"Who are you?" a single voice demanded.

"*We are the race of lantyn*," came the reply.

"Whom do you serve?"

"*The dragons are our masters,*

We, their willing slaves –"

Don't listen! Ada closed her eyes and clenched her fists. She dared not try to block her ears in case she upset her hair and there were only a few minutes left now.

A swarm of butterflies were going berserk inside her. Her heart was beating itself black and blue against her ribcage. Did cliff divers feel like this before leaping off the precipice? Only she presumed they had a choice in the matter. Her only choice was to proceed with dignity or to melt down and disgrace herself.

"Breathe in, breathe out and don't forget to pout."

Startled, Ada looked down.

Meruda grinned up at her; the dark crinkles around her mouth intensified her mischievous air. One eyelid glinted as it flickered a wink. Then she was head down once more, fussing with yet another final touch, while she noisily sucked great lungfuls of air in and out with pointed meaning.

A reluctant smile tugged at Ada's lips. She inhaled deep and slow.

Her hand trailed over the glossy blue material of her dress, trying to luxuriate in its silky splendour. She couldn't. Her sense of touch was totally desensitised by the thick layers of irilda oil which had been liberally applied to her skin, and not just her skin but the fabric of the dress as well. She longed to scrape away the grease but that would never do. The stuff was more valuable than gold and its unique properties were essential to her father's plans for tonight.

"Do you think it will work?" Ada asked, eyeing her distorted reflection on the polished surface of a floor-standing candelabra. Overall, the picture was reassuring: her coppery-brown hair was elegantly fashioned with a few long ringlets framing her neck and her crystal skin glinted bright. Unlike Meruda, her crystal skin was only marked with a faint marbling, the pattern of water. Some poor people were born with dark streaks, coloured mottling, pockmarks or even plain lumpiness, but there was nothing common or plain about her reflection and it was offset beautifully by the cascading folds of the glistening dress.

"Breathing and pouting?" Meruda asked. "Well it always seems to make you laugh when I do it."

Ada suppressed a snort. "I meant the dress."

"Oh that. It had better. I've been slaving over it for weeks and you've been imprisoned in it for hours already."

Her last few words rang out uncomfortably loud. Silence had fallen outside. It was time.

"My lords and ladies," the words were muted by the great oak doors but quite distinct. They were announcing her entry.

Ada bit her lip. *Not yet*, she pleaded with the wooden face of the grand doors. *Not yet, I'm not ready.*

A voice spoke from behind her. "You should take your maid's advice and breathe."

Ada stiffened.

Meruda bowed her head and withdrew.

Taking a slow, deep breath, Ada turned around. She didn't look up but fixed her gaze on the floorboards as she curtsied.

He came and circled her. Her father.

Her stomach gave a nasty jolt. He must have overheard her doubts about the dress. Was he angry?

She listened to his footsteps pass around her, step back and pause. She could feel his judicial eye burning into her, assessing his investment.

It wasn't fair. It might be childish to think so but it was true. For him, tonight was just another opportunity to show off his wealth and power, one more move in his endless power game. She hated being used like this. When would he see her for herself and not as a pawn?

His silence grew heavy. He was probably testing her now, playing a game with her without telling her the rules. All the bitter, well-nursed grievances of her life welled up until she felt ready to explode.

His feet finished the circle and came to a standstill in front of her own, mirroring her position.

Sudden dread withered her fire. Ada felt sick.

"You look beautiful."

Startled, she looked up. He wasn't exactly smiling (then again, he never did) but there was a rare softness in his ice-blue eyes. Her father, the Lord Dura, did not waste words: if he said it, he meant it and often a good deal more.

Ada felt her cheeks flush in an uncontrollable flood of relief and pleasure. She tried to say something nice back but couldn't find the right words.

With a sudden heave, the doors began to open.

He moved to stand alongside her, offering her his hand. "Stand tall now. Remember who you are."

She took his hand. Finally, they were literally standing side-by-side for the Dura honour, working together. She would not disappoint him.

Music slipped through the opening doors in a soft, yet majestic melody. A warm tingle spread over Ada's skin. She braced herself.

"How is it?" he asked in an even, almost disinterested, tone.

Ada glanced down at her hand and the dress, watching the blue light shimmer into existence. The irilda fire flower reacted to music; so now its oil shone. Soon she was glowing like a living star.

Kessler had once said that brides used irildas to symbolise that their lantyn hearts were pure and full of light, but that it took the average commoner several years of saving up before they could afford a single flower. Ada shook the thought away, uncomfortably aware that the fortune she was dressed in would send out a rather different message.

She waggled her luminescent fingers, conscious that the sensation was growing less pleasant as the music grew louder, but she only said, "It's bearable, just a prickle."

"Good. Let's go." He led her out.

The cool summer night air rushed around her, carrying the melody with stronger resonance, causing the irilda oil to burn more brightly. Ada could hear the appreciative murmurs and gasps from the guests on the lower terraces, could feel their watching eyes, but she could no longer see them. The glowing oil on her face had created a dazzling ring around the complete periphery of her vision and everything was reduced to blocked-out silhouettes, devoid of detail.

It didn't matter: her father was leading her forward slowly and she knew what would be happening ahead. At the centre of the terrace, a dragnoss guardian would be muttering over the betrothal beacon, asking for the dragons' approval, while Rishard il Frénore approached from the other end of the terrace. Irilda buds, which had been painstakingly slotted among the ivy that climbed the house behind them, would be unfurling at the sound of music, blossoming into fully fledged fire-flowers and tugging themselves free to float up into the night sky.

The music started to crescendo, swelling to a climax and with it the light from the irilda oil intensified, and the growing irritation on Ada's skin ignited into a scorching burn. Ada fought the urge to scratch and itch and shriek or anything else that might make the pain more endurable. She couldn't even clench her fist or teeth for fear the crowd would notice. She slowly sucked in a long breath, pushing her shoulders back, straightening her back and raising her chin, determined to look the part. One moment more…

Her father pulled slightly at her hand, indicating they should halt.

Silence.

It was blissful. The moment the music stopped the burning ceased too. The light hadn't vanished as fast (there was still a fading glow) but its accompanying prickle was scarcely noticeable. Ada released a quiet sigh. She blinked twice, willing her sight to return into focus and identify the surrounding figures. Within a few moments she could make them out: to her left stood Callum, the Chief of the Dragnoss Guardians, with his entourage of white-clad attendants and just opposite her, not an arm span away, stood Rishard il Frénore. He smiled warmly.

Ada smiled back without thinking.

"Lantyns of Aven," Callum boomed. "We gather to witness a pledging before the dragons as Lord Dura gives his daughter, the Lady Ada il Dura, in betrothal to the Count of Frénore."

Ada swallowed, but she felt calm. It was as if the irilda oil had burnt away all her anxiety and she could think again.

"Tonight, they light their betrothal beacon, and if the dragons favour us and their hearts prove true, we will return in a year's time to celebrate their marriage."

A year. She had a year before it was all settled. Not that she really had a choice.

"Ada il Dura, take the man your father has chosen."

Callum indicated that she should take hold of the torch that Rishard was holding. As she placed her hand above his, Rishard stretched his thumb to gently squeeze her fingers. It was strongly mottled against her clear skin.

Her father's choice...

"I charge you both to use this year wisely. It is a time for solemn reflection –"

Why Rishard? A middle-ranking nobleman was hardly a politically prudent choice.

She looked at him more closely. He had changed, filling out since she had last seen him three years ago and, unlike his thumb, his facial crystal was almost purer than hers. He caught her eye and the corner of his mouth slid up a fraction, just as it had when they were children silently revelling in a shared secret. A knot in her chest – one she hadn't even been aware of until that moment – loosened. She remembered that she had rather liked Rishard. It had been her inescapable duty to accept whoever her father chose, however ghastly the choice, but he had chosen Rishard for her. Warmth tingled her tummy.

"– and may you know the dragons' help."

Ada turned with Rishard and, hands overlapping, they lit the betrothal beacon. The flames licked up into the night.

"My lords and ladies, I present the betrothed pair of Frénore and Dura."

Amid the eruption of applause and fanfares, Ada and Rishard slowly descended wide stone steps lined by ivory saplings, down towards the lower terrace. The trumpet blasts sparked the irilda oil into fresh, albeit fainter life, but

Ada ignored the itching burn and fixed her expression into a gracious smile as she nodded at one unknown face after another, determined to look the part.

They reached the large stone patio and the crowd backed away. Rishard led her to the centre of the space and into position for the first dance. The minstrels started to play and then played as if they never meant to stop. Before she knew it, Ada was surrounded and trapped by a whirling mass of colour, forcing her to continue. No sooner had the first dance finished than the next one began, then a third and a fourth; it was all one long nightmare of convoluted footwork.

Ada's thoughts spun out of time with the dances. She found herself both longing and dreading to be alone with Rishard. It was all very well smiling at each other until their cheeks ached, but what was he like? He might be a completely different person to the boy she had once known. Not that they had spent that much time together, only one summer, but who was he now? Who had he become? They hadn't even managed to say one full sentence to each other yet. He could be...anything.

Fireworks exploded. Crackling sky-fizzers: red, gold, blue, silver, a thousand falling shards of light – it was breathtaking. After the first titanic explosion, Ada glanced at Rishard and met his eye. He jerked his head slightly towards the edge of the dance floor. She nodded and they fled from the scene in perfect synchrony.

They found a more secluded spot in one of the vine walkways that branched off from the lower terraces. Rishard kept trying to speak but his attempts were so hopelessly drowned out that they reached a mimed agreement to wait until the end of the display.

Eventually the last thunderous boom faded. Rishard turned to her. "I hope –"

"Frénore!" A boyish-faced nobleman ambushed them, clapping Rishard on the back.

"Laurence!" Rishard returned the gesture and turned beaming to Ada. "Ada, this is my good friend Laurence Halbert, third son of Lord and Lady Kishere. Laurence, allow me to present my betrothed, Lady Ada il Dura."

He sounded so pleased and proud that Ada felt quite peculiar. Did he mean that, or was she just a trophy to boast about? And did he expect her to feel like that about him? She couldn't, of course she couldn't: she hardly knew him. Besides, the betrothal was her duty and doorway to status, and to demand romance demonstrated a lack of self-control. Yet Rishard's glowing gaze confused her. She liked it.

After some initial congratulations, Rishard and Laurence resumed a friendly argument they had evidently started earlier. They were soon joined by Rishard's cousin, Fillipe, who made a few attempts to involve Ada in the debate, but he was soon too entangled himself to help her. Ada waited as patiently as she could, but it was soon clear that they would be happy to spend the whole night disputing the various merits of different armours. After saying less than three words in what felt like an hour, she had had more than enough.

"If you'll excuse me gentlemen..."

Fillipe turned to give her a cursory nod but then rejoined the conversation. Rishard and Laurence didn't even stop talking.

Ada slipped away disappointed.

She took care not to get cornered by anyone, keeping in the shadows and skirting the crowd as much as possible. Her feet groaned at each step, but she kept up her purposeful pace so that people would think that she couldn't stop. Within a few minutes she had managed to slip back into the house and into their private quarters, find a dark, secluded corner with an inviting chaise lounge upon which she collapsed with relief.

Any lingering guilt for abandoning Rishard soon evaporated. He was clearly enjoying himself and she needed to sit down. Why didn't they have chairs at these balls? Surely, she couldn't be the only one with aching feet?

Ada shut her eyes and leant her head back with a sigh, savouring the peace and delicious solitude...until whispers punctured the silence.

3

Foxes and Squirrels

Their voices were soft, indistinct, like a running stream.

Ada frowned. No-one else should be back here. The guests should be on the terraces or dispersed in the grounds and surely the servants wouldn't dare linger in this part of the house, for fear of being missed.

Intruders? She held her breath, paralysed.

The trickle of conversation paused and started again. Yes, it was coming from indoors and close by.

The noise was strangely reassuring. After all, how many assassins stopped to chat? If not assassins then who, thieves? Or plotting courtiers? Of course, she could slip back to the safety of the crowd, and ask Kessler to investigate or accompany her, but Kessler was hardly the stealthy type. Besides it might be nothing more than a couple of slacking servants and the thought that anyone might find out that she had needed a bodyguard to confront domestics was mortifying.

After a moment of agonised indecision Ada got up and crept towards the sound, laying one foot slowly down before the other, almost walking sideways to stop her dress rustling. She peered through the gloomy passageway. Outside, in the gardens, the summer night had been set ablaze with lanterns and flaming torches, but these more private areas of the house were fuzzy with dimness, since her father did not believe in "needless extravagance".

Odd phrases broke free from the inaudible flow.

"...more than one..."

"...can't work in the dark."

"...difficulty trusting..."

She reached the corner leading into the grand reception hall and paused. As the main entrance to their house, it was well lit by an abundance of beeswax candles. Any further and they would easily see her, whoever they were. Ada leant forward, straining to catch the words. They were clearer now.

"...eggs in one basket."

"I understand, but you can't expect -"

"Lady Ada!" Kessler's voice resounded through the corridors.

There was a quick scuffle of alarm from around the corner. Ada darted forward, hoping to catch a glimpse of them, only to stumble over the hem of her dress and surge out into the hallway, arms flailing in cartwheels as she fought to regain her balance. She succeeded. Just.

The double doors of the front entrance were ajar. From the shadows of the outer courtyard, movement winked and was gone, but someone remained. A solitary man stood in the hallway. He remained facing the doors, his back to Ada, his hands on his hips in an easy, lordly manner. His green doublet, embroidered with gold thread, caught the candlelight and set him in stark contrast to the blackness beyond.

Before anything could happen, Kessler called for her again, his voice closer, now edged with a subtle impatience.

Good, she wouldn't be alone for long.

At the sound of Kessler's second call, the man had jumped with overdone surprise and swivelled around. He smiled. "My dear Lady Ada," he purred. "What in the realm are you doing out here? You should be back among your guests, enjoying the night."

It wasn't what he said, or even how he said it, but there was an air of mockery in his words. Ada suddenly felt very small and silly.

"I could ask you the same question," she replied, stalling.

He looked like a courtier although she did not know his face. Not that that meant much. All evening she had felt woefully ignorant, unable to match the great names of court to their respective owners. She couldn't help feeling that this was a significant gap in her education – one that her father could have easily prevented. Even the simplest description would have sufficed to identify this gentleman: those dark, criss-crossing lines marring the crystal skin over his cheekbones were most distinctive, especially in the way they compacted at either side of his face when his mouth widened into a smile; for he was smiling most genially, and with each step of his leisurely approach, the smile seemed to widen another fraction.

"After all," Ada pursued, "you *are* one of the guests I presume. And I am curious as to why you aren't enjoying the night with the rest?"

He chuckled. "An excellent point. I am afraid that – ah, Master Kessler, is it not?"

Ada had felt, rather than seen, the steward's arrival, but his presence had not reassured her as she had hoped: he radiated alarm. Kessler was an open book to her (unlike her father) and since he was rarely perturbed by anything, his apprehension now was unnerving.

The steward gave a stiff bow. "Forgive me for intruding, but Count Frénore was looking for his betrothed –"

"Oh well, don't let me detain –" the stranger began but Kessler had not stopped talking and continued to speak over the other's interjection: "– as the boat is ready. Will you come too sir or do you prefer the festivities out here?"

A cold frost stole over the other man's smile. "My, my. I didn't expect impudence from you. I was told Dura's steward was a soft touch."

Silence hovered.

"But," the genial warmth returned, "you are quite right. Forgive me, I was merely ensuring my groom was ready for a swift departure. I will be leaving early, as an unavoidable business matter has cropped up. My apologies Lady Ada for such rudeness, especially at your engagement ball."

"Unavoidable business matters are, by definition, unavoidable. Shall we?" Ada asked, turning back towards the garden.

"Indeed, we shall." He approached and offered her his arm. "My lady."

Refusal was unthinkable. He slithered a limb around her waist, pinioning her to himself like a prize possession he was determined to keep hold of. Indeed, when they reached the garden door, he even tried to pull her forward and publicly escort her outside but Ada pulled herself free.

"You'll excuse me sir, but I must speak with my steward."

The man gave her one last knowing smile, bowed and sauntered into the crowds.

"Well done, my lady," Kessler breathed, worry ageing his face as he eyed the retreating figure. "What your father would have said if he'd seen you coming out with him, I dread to think. That man is pure, brazen cunning. Shameless."

"But who was he?"

Kessler looked startled. "You don't know?"

"Would I ask if I did?" It was difficult not to snap. Kessler, for all his good qualities, could be infuriatingly slow.

"Of course, forgive me, my lady. That was the Baron Ashilda."

Ada blinked. She peered back around the corner to see the said Baron laughing among a group of nobles. Cold prickled her spine.

"Well!" she exhaled. "I'm glad you arrived when you did. Now what is this about a boat?"

"It's something your father has arranged. Speaking of which, I need to tell him about this incident. What was the Baron doing? And how –?"

“There you are.” Meruda came bustling in through the garden doors. “I hope, my lady, you weren’t going out on the water without this.” She unfurled a summer cloak (deep blue to complement the dress), neatly draped it over Ada’s shoulders and bobbed a curtsy to Kessler, all in one fluid movement. “My deepest apologies for interrupting you, master steward,” she said, fluttering her eyelids.

“I...er...” Kessler looked at Ada, desperation in his eyes.

“You had better get back to your other duties,” Ada said, hiding a smile.

Kessler jerked his head and beat a hasty retreat.

Ada fought to keep a straight face until he was gone. “You shouldn’t do that,” she scolded Meruda, her voice gurgling with laughter.

“Do what?” Meruda responded in wide-eyed innocence.

“Make Kessler uncomfortable like that. No, don’t argue, I've been here long enough already.” She arranged her features into her prettiest smile and sallied out into the social torment.

She was instantly swallowed up by the sea of smiling faces, submerged under their flattery or hearty laughs; lost in the swirling maze of colour and music. Why had she ever wanted a ball held in her honour? She could no longer skulk at the side to watch or withdraw whenever she wanted, but was subject to this ceaseless bombardment of goodwill. More importantly, she had to respond correctly to every well-wisher, hiding with an easy smile her frenzied efforts to match faces to titles and dredge up suitable details about each. Yet that was how power-play worked: she must learn this game, no matter how exhausting.

Meeting Lady Marguerite il Kishere was a vast relief. She was sensible, sympathetic and easy to talk to, yet no sooner had Ada begun to enjoy herself than Lady Jemina il Ashilda invaded the conversation. Lady Jemina seemed to be part-limpet, impervious to snubs, and never stopped her gushing condescension.

"Of course, irildas are traditional and that was a pretty little display you put on, so shiny and all that, but irildas don't have any real scent and scent lasts a lot longer than a quick flash of light. Elipmnus nard now – what a fragrance! It is to die for. You have never tried it I suppose, but not to worry: I will send you some or you can visit me – whenever you like – and then you will agree that it is superior in every way."

"Is it really?" Ada could scarcely believe her ears. Lady Marguerite looked bemused too. Evidently, she, unlike Lady Jemina, knew that Lord Dura virtually owned the Isle of Elipmnus and consequently the trade in its nard. Yet nothing could stop Lady Jemina: she launched into a long-winded and erroneous explanation of everything to do with the island and its fabled nard. Ada wished she had been more sarcastic, but felt that Lady Jemina would have carried on talking regardless. Even Lady Marguerite seemed unable to quell the garrulous flow.

Ada felt a scream threatening to emerge *How much more of this did she have to go through? Where was Rishard?* She thought he was meant to be waiting for her.

"Ada?"

He had stepped out of nowhere, as if in answer to her thoughts, his voice noticeable because of its quietness. He placed an arm around her waist, overrode Lady Jemina with a jovial apology, nodded respectfully to Lady Marguerite and drew Ada through the crowd, shielding her from all further conversation with a profusion of polite excuses to the passing guests. Ada followed his lead eagerly, her gratitude marred by irritation at his delay.

Within minutes they had reached the waterside. Rishard and Ada clambered into the central seat, a servant took up the punt and, in another moment, they were skimming out over the inky waters, alone. Very alone: theirs was the only boat.

It occurred to her that Rishard had left some space between them on the seat and hadn't said a word. He answered her glance. "Don't talk until you want to: enjoy the respite from socialising torture."

Ada smiled her thanks and savoured the tranquillity.

This little break in the punt was the best idea her father had had in years. It had come just in time to save her from madness, murder or possibly both.

Music resonated over the water's surface but the noise was made gentle by the distance. For a few moments the gentle lapping of the water against the side of the boat was the loudest sound to be heard. You would scarcely know that you were in Casida. Ada could almost imagine that she was back home in Ilnora, crossing the river...almost, but not quite. Even with her eyes shut she could sense that this was little more than an oversized pond, a pseudo lake fed by one of those many underground tunnels that channelled the River Rinnoir through the city.

The tunnels...Ada shuddered at the recent events.

"Are you all right?" Rishard eyed her with concern.

Ada pulled herself together and nodded. She might tell Rishard about her kidnap, in fact she wanted to, but not with her father's servant listening in the background.

They bumped into the quay of the ornamental island, moored the boat and began to wander along the stone-paved path towards the bench. The servant followed them carrying a lantern. Rishard waved him back.

"I'm sorry sir, but I must accompany you."

"Yes, yes, modesty forbid! But do you have to do it with that beacon? If everyone can still watch us, we might as well have stayed on the terrace."

Reluctantly, the servant covered the lantern, but he followed them even more closely than before, and once they were seated, he positioned himself directly behind them.

Ada felt her heart beat a bit faster. What was she supposed to do now? What did Rishard expect from her? She waited.

A new display of paper-lantern puppet kites rose into the night sky. Animals, both exotic and familiar, paraded mid-air, their reflections dancing over the dark waters.

"Well," Rishard eventually started, "it is good to be alone with you."

"Yes."

The servant's steady breathing dominated the soundscape.

"It's been a long time."

"Yes," she replied again, wishing she could think of something more intelligent. They doubtless wouldn't get many opportunities like this (chaperoned or not) and she needed to make the most of it.

Thankfully Rishard beat her to it. "I know this is somewhat awkward," he burst out. "Us, I mean, particularly for you. I asked for this but you didn't. But I don't want...well actually I *do* want..." He stopped, flushing. "What I'm trying to say is, let's start by being friends."

For the first time in what felt like hours, Ada smiled without having to think about it. A flustered Rishard was a new sight, so different from the suave manner he had worn all evening that it gave sincerity to his words. She savoured the moment. Yet relief superseded pleasure. She wouldn't have to act with him, or conjure up feelings she didn't have yet. They could enjoy being friends, and as for the future, she would hope for the best.

"Well, if we are only friends," she began, "don't you think we looked a little too eager to sail away together?"

"You did seem a little hasty," he said in a voice of sombre reproof, although his lips twitched.

"And I suppose nearly dragging me away didn't look too good either."

"Yes," he agreed in mock woe. "We're hardly fit for court life. We better send His Majesty our apologies for tomorrow."

Ada suddenly shivered. With all the excitement tonight, she had forgotten about being presented to the king tomorrow.

Rishard appeared to sense her unease and gave her an uncertain pat on the back. Ada smiled to herself at his awkwardness.

"It's not that bad," he reassured her. "His Majesty has a sense of humour and there are quite a few characters at court. Why, Lord Rothford –"

"Another crowd of strangers to smile at and pretend to be delighted to meet." She shuffled her feet, wondering if she dared rest her head on his shoulder. She didn't. "It is strange, but all those years growing up secluded at Ilnora, surrounded by peasants, squirrels and foxes, I longed for the glamour of court life, and now I'm here..."

"You can't wait to go back home," he said softly.

She looked up at his face, "Oh I didn't mean away from *you*. I only meant –"

"I know," he said, smiling. "You just miss home and Casida is very different. I miss the south too; that blend of warmth and cool sea breezes. At least Kessler came with you. I remember him from when we met at Humberstone as children: he caught me in the apple barrel – do you remember? You pleaded clemency and he listened. You were always good friends."

Ada smiled, pleased to have someone understand.

"Yes. Father relieved him of his duties managing our southern estates just so he could be here tonight. Sometimes –" She stopped short. It wouldn't do for her to say that she considered Kessler more as a foster father than a steward, particularly with a servant present. Yet it was the truth. For as long as she could remember he had been there, watching over her, advising, chiding and caring for her, much more present than her own father had been. She hesitated, uncertain how to finish her sentence.

Rishard appeared not to notice. "Well, you have Kessler and me, and just to make it feel like home, some foxes as well."

"Foxes?"

Rishard nodded to the shore where the newest puppet-kite, a glorious red fox, had climbed into the sky, chasing its tail. She rolled her eyes and elbowed him in the ribs. He laughed.

The invisible watcher viewed the festivities from the roof in frozen stillness. Its taloned feet were wrapped firmly around the stone parapet with both wings slightly raised, constantly ready to take off. Only its tail twitched as it looked down at Ada.

4

Choice

So...it had all been for nothing.

Kelvin stared at the dead-end gully; his dead end.

A chorus of hunting horns echoed across the valley behind. The noise was almost gleeful. They knew they had him cornered.

His knees shook, buckled and gave way. Orla slipped from his arms. He fumbled to catch her but only succeeded in rolling her into the long grass and alpine flowers. She uttered one sleepy half-cry, briefly arched her spine like a cat and relaxed back into sleep, lost in child dreamland.

He didn't need to worry about Orla. They would take good care of her, even revere her as a goldenhead, no matter what her parents had done. His own fate would be quite another matter.

The short, sharp clarion blasts sounded again, nearer this time. The patrols were converging, closing in. He didn't have much time.

Kelvin quickly surveyed his surroundings, looking around at the clearing, behind at the pine trees and up at the vindictive cliffs that hemmed him in, trying to work out the best method. It needed to be something instant: he did not want to risk still being alive when they found him. He would not be rescued only to undergo Saupa's exacting sense of vengeful justice.

He got up. From this standing perspective he could see some sharp stones at the base of a cliff, fallen from a scree slope higher up. Yes...he could use them. Kelvin took a wobbly step forward.

A bizarre, giddy excitement began to bubble up inside him. He was in control now; the master of his own fate at last, even if it was to be such a fate at least it was of his choosing. He would cheat them all. He would –

"Shoo!"

Kelvin jumped. Orla had woken and was sitting bolt-upright, her four-and-a-half-year-old face screwed up into a stern scowl, looking beyond him. "Shoo!" she said again.

Despite himself, Kelvin glanced over his shoulder to see what she was looking at. There was nothing there. He turned back to Orla only to find that she was midway through an enormous yawn without the slightest sign of alarm. Even once she had finished yawning, she merely flashed Kelvin a smile and picked an alpine flower.

"Orla, what were you shooing?" Kelvin asked, voice low, cautiously scanning the treeline Orla faced.

"I didn't like the dragon." She spoke as if seeing a dragon was the most normal thing in the world.

"Dragon?" Kelvin echoed, bewildered.

"It was whooshing dark clouds into you, so I told it to shoo. Mama says "shoo" to Pecky when she strays into the hut. Pecky is my hen and I chose her when she was a chick – but she should live out and not in."

"Right," Kelvin said distractedly as the horns sounded again, louder this time, closer. The wood was empty as far as he could see. Perhaps she hadn't seen anything and the dragon was merely part of a waking dream.

Orla began to hum tunelessly, picking off the petals one by one. The sun broke through the grey clouds, filling the dell with sudden warmth and catching Orla's crystal skin. She shone softly. Her hair wafted around her head in a golden halo.

He shook himself. If he was going to do anything he needed to do it now. He wondered if she would stay here if he told her to, even when he didn't come back? What if she found his body before the patrol could find her and take her away?

Once more he started towards the cliff, less certain now. Orla got up and followed him, hopping from one patch of long grass to another, giggling and chattering about how it swished and tickled.

The horns-blasts rang even nearer.

Kelvin was suddenly filled with indecision. Death had been easier to consider when Orla had been sleeping but now...He reached the grey cliff face and put a hand on a lichen-covered outcrop. He hesitated in an agony of indecision.

"Where's mama?"

Kelvin's heart sank. He thought she had understood, but she was so young, maybe too young to understand about death. He crouched down to look into Orla's face. "She's gone to be with Yhari," he said gently.

Orla cocked her head frowning. "Does Yhari have Damkash tea? Because Mama said she didn't think life would be worth living without a good cup of Damkash with friends. I know Yhari is her friend but has he got Damkash tea?"

"I...er...I don't know." Kelvin turned away and slid down to sit with his back against the rock, a sudden lump constricting his throat.

He felt a hand being laid on his shoulder. "Is *your* mama with Yhari?"

Bless her. He tried to smile. "I suppose so. Yes. And my papa. They went a long time ago."

"I'm sorry. They could meet my family and say hello."

How did she manage it? After all the horrors of the last week, how could she be so calm and certain? She was so young. He was her senior by more than a decade, had witnessed dealings in the imperial court, had been personally trained by arguably the most influential philosopher in Nordlann, and yet he had less conviction in his whole body than this peasant toddler had in her little finger. It may be a mere unreasoning childish belief on her part, but its effect was enviable.

The first faint signs of shouting reached his ear. Not long now. He couldn't do it in front of her, but the alternative...

"I'm going to climb the ladder."

Ladder? Kelvin started up.

It wasn't a ladder as such, more a deep crack in the rock face, filled with compacted dirt in a series of levels like steps. It was tucked further around this outcrop, invisible when viewed face-on as he had, but Orla had evidently been more adventurous. In fact, she had already reached his head height. She stumbled. Kelvin rushed in and up to steady her. She laughed and hauled herself further up.

Kelvin hastily followed, one arm always outstretched, full of agonised terror that she would fall.

He followed step by step, eyes flicking between the treeline, the ground below, to Orla and the thread-like path they were following. So long as it went high enough and they kept out the patrol's sight they had a chance – just a chance – that they could escape and make it over the border.

He couldn't give up.

He had to get Orla to safety.

He had to find Dura.

5

The Dragons of Silver

Ada had a headache. A pulse niggled behind her left eye, she felt slightly sick and, worst of all, was terrified of losing her balance and toppling into the dragnoss – the yawning chasm before her. The sticky-sweet concoction Meruda had given her to help with the pain might have succeeded in numbing the stabbing in her skull, but its alchemy had miscarried as far as her legs were concerned and had turned them into lead. Not the best preparation for perching on the brink of an abyss.

The festivities had finished only a few hours ago, the last guest leaving as the first traces of dawn had streaked the sky. As soon as they were all gone her father had packed her off to bed. Ada didn't know why he had bothered: by the time Meruda and the others had managed to undo her hair and release her from that gown, it was time to start getting dressed up in a fresh lot of finery, ready for a new day of ritual and formality.

Of course, on such a day as this, the very first thing to do was to visit the dragnoss. Custom demanded they give a tribute to the dragons for every major life event, and a betrothal was certainly that. She felt a twinge of guilt, knowing that she hadn't yet given something after that miraculous escape from her kidnapping, but to do so would have guaranteed her father hearing of the incident. As he had remained silent on the subject, she was beginning to believe the unbelievable: he didn't know.

"Count Frénore and Lady Dura, please step forward with your gifts."

Aren't we close enough already? Ada's heart surged into a hammering sprint.

They were all waiting for her. Meruda was poised with the unfolded cloth, proffering the gift Ada had chosen – a silver brooch of a twisting dragon studded with sapphires – while Rishard watched her, his fat purse ready in his palm.

Ada shook herself, half-angry that she was so nervous. She must not show weakness: now was the time to prove herself. She was not a drooping flower or fragile decoration: she would stand tall and shoulder this and all the other duties her father had never thought it worthwhile to train her for. She would show herself a worthy daughter of the house of Dura. Ada straightened her back.

She picked up the piece of jewellery and forced herself forward. Her legs responded slowly. Ada dropped her shoulders and swayed gently, hoping to transform her sluggishness into languid grace. She wondered how successful she was.

As she came alongside Rishard, she took his hand, interlocking her fingers tightly with his. The soles of her feet tingled at the sight of the drop. They always prickled at great heights, but this was a precipice to a different world: a portal to the Dragons' Realm. Somewhere in that darkness, hidden deep below, the dragons lived in their world of fire and light and all that stood between them and that monstrous drop was the short perimeter wall.

Ada gazed into the dragnoss. This was no natural chasm: all was smooth. Its rim formed a giant oval and the polished sides ended in a clean edge after only a spear's length down. Nothingness lurked beyond. It almost looked like a large pool of perfectly still, black liquid. Yet there were no ripples when tribute was dropped into it: whatever you offered simply fell down, down, down...until the darkness swallowed it forever.

Rishard pinched her.

Ada found that she was leaning dangerously far forward, drawn to gaze at those hypnotic depths. She righted herself and shuffled back.

She breathed him a thank you, not daring to move her lips. The presiding dragnoss guardian had just stepped up onto the podium on the opposite edge, a mere stone's throw away (her stone's throw away at any rate; she dared say that Rishard could manage twice the distance).

"Be generous to the dragons with your bounty."

At his sonorous tones the crowd of tribute-givers encircling the dragnoss stilled into silence. Movement still flowed around the edges of the vast circular chamber, as others hurried on with their own business, but everyone maintained a respectful hush. All the various classes and breeds of people, whether they had come to offer tribute themselves (or pickpocket other people's tribute before they reached the dragnoss) or simply to have a peek at the nobility's fancy clothes, all fell dumb before a guardian's soliloquy.

"Give without restraint, for it symbolises the treasure of your hearts, which the dragons love even more than gold and silver..."

Ada struggled to listen. It was not the type of address she was used to. Back in Ilnora, Guardian Rosquebelle would vivaciously tell of the dragon fables, briefly state its meaning and invite discussion. Of course, things were very different in Ilnora: there was no terrifying chasm for one thing (any tribute offered was regularly collected, delivered and offered on their behalf by the guardians). Moreover, for all his kindly rambling, Guardian Rosquebelle didn't inflict meaningless blather on anyone. It was impossible to concentrate on the current drivel, especially when feeling like a metal band was clamped tightly around your skull. She let the words wash over her, the odd phrase penetrating her consciousness.

"...allegorical representation of deepest truth...Opening our hearts to that promise...The gift of the light of life..."

Dragons' breath! Were they always so long-winded?

She felt dizzy and slightly nauseous. She found herself swaying and tightened her grasp on Rishard's arm. He pressed it back in silent reassurance.

Not daring to look down again, Ada looked up, fixing her eyes on the huge silver sculpture of Levia, the mother dragon of Aven. It was suspended from the distant domed roof, hung by fantastically long metal chains, so that Mother Levia seemed to endlessly hover above the chasm. Alongside her were wisp-like figurines representing sirens, the mysterious and beautiful creatures who could see the secrets of your heart. It was said that the dragons sent them to guide lantyns in times of trouble...it was said. Ada had lost count of the times when, as a child, she had put her money in a tribute box, shut her eyes and wished to see a siren. She never had, but that didn't stop the beauty of the thought or hope.

Ada imagined the figurines moving in a grand dance.

"Now my lord and lady it is time to present your gifts and lead us all in the offering of tribute."

Finally.

In unison, Ada and Rishard outstretched their arms and released. Ada felt a stab of sadness as she watched her sapphire clasp disappearing into the depths for ever. Tribute was meant to hold emotional as well as monetary value, and this clasp had both in abundance. So much so that she was annoyed by the impersonal shower of coins from Rishard's upturned purse. They made it difficult to follow the descent of her silver dragon, but within moments nothing more could be seen of anything. All of it had faded out of sight, beyond them forever.

"Well, there goes another good bit of gold down the hole," Rishard said, a few minutes later when the carriage rumbled its way off to Vière Castle, the royal residence at the heart of Casida. He had settled himself opposite Ada (looking infuriatingly fresh) while Meruda sat in silent attendance beside her.

Ada's heart sank at his bouncing tone. She did not feel up to badinage.

"You better not let my father hear you," she replied. "He will forbid the marriage and have you hounded out of the country for dragon treason."

"I doubt it," Rishard's grin widened. "He'd be more likely to give me a stern warning about speaking so freely. He'd say something about the guardians holding too much power for anyone to complain about paying them tribute. Of course, he'd be right, but that doesn't make it any easier for me to throw my gold down for them."

Ada smiled to herself. It was just the sort of thing her father would say.

"Our tribute," she responded, "is for the dragons, not the guardians."

"Honestly Ada, no-one really gives the dragons anything." His air of superiority was maddening. "All our gold, silver and jewels vanish down a hole in the ground for creatures that no-one has ever seen and the guardians inexplicably manage to live in luxury and wealth. But no-one dares stop giving just in case the dragons are real."

"Is that why you gave today? Just in case?"

He grinned even wider. "Oh no. I keep giving because your father happens to be right. It would create too many difficulties if I stopped. That's why most people carry on with it. Just think what a scandal we would have caused if we neglected giving tribute after our betrothal."

"So, you don't believe the dragons are real at all?"

"I would be a fool to say that dragons do not exist."

"That is not at all the same thing."

His eyes twinkled. "I know."

The carriage tilted back as they crossed a bridge. Ada glanced down into the exposed water channel below.

"What is it?" Rishard asked. "You had that look on your face in the punt last night. What is it about the water?"

Ada took the plunge and told him about the kidnapping incident and her reluctance to tell her father.

"I see." Rishard drummed his fingers, frowning in thought. He nodded at Meruda. "It appears that you and I are the privileged few whom Lady Ada trusts."

Meruda murmured agreement.

Rishard snapped his fingers. "Sniffer!"

Ada and Meruda jumped. "What did you say?" Ada asked.

"I'll get my man Sniffer to look into it. He has a way of ferreting out information, and don't worry; he'll be discreet."

"Thank you."

"Not at all: I want to make sure that I'm the only one who ever sweeps you off your feet."

Ada smiled weakly in response, but it was good to know that someone would investigate the episode. Maybe now she could stop worrying every time she spotted an entrance to the river tunnels; the city was riddled with them.

Their conversation dwindled into companionable silence. Ada was thankful. She had not wanted to tell Rishard to be quiet, but her head...

She closed her eyes and let her mind relax.

"Ada."

Did he have to start talking so soon?

"Ada, we're at the gates."

She blearily opened her eyes, then started upright, heart racing.

Rishard laughed. "No need to panic, we've still a few moments. Did you enjoy your nap?"

"What nap?"

He laughed again. "No need to pretend. I understand."

Perhaps he did, but she wasn't in the mood to be patronised. Ada wasn't sure what to make of Rishard: one moment he seemed tender, thoughtful and pleasant to be with, the next he was highhanded, as if he knew everything. But it was early days yet; in time she would learn how to read and anticipate him, she thought.

She looked out of the window, grateful that her headache had eased as she squinted up at the towering castle walls that pierced the bright summer sky. Vière Castle was decidedly flamboyant: hundreds of airy windows with ornate lintels sat in neat rows amid smooth grey stones, and the number of pointed, blue-slated turrets was frankly ridiculous. She liked it: much prettier than the solid, thick-set defensive strongholds her father favoured.

He was here now, stepping forward to meet their slowing carriage, with Rishard's cousin Fillipe beside him, ready to represent the Frénore family. Behind them both lurked the starchy-faced Callum. As the guardian who had overseen their betrothal it was only right that he should be the one to officially present them to the king on behalf of the dragons, but Ada didn't much care for him. He had a large, pale face and his glass skin had a lumpy look, like butter which had partially melted and solidified. He gave them a thin-lipped smile of welcome and the lumps slid to either side of his face. Ada was thankful when he turned to lead the way indoors.

She had to blink hard to adjust her eyes from the outside brightness, but once she could see she hardly knew where to look first. Brightly-painted floor tiles spread out before her and climbed the wide stairs ahead; tall columns stretched up to the vaulted ceiling which were painted with frescos that made Ada want to fly; and mirrorstone sculptures set into the wall recesses glistened like ice carvings, depicting heroic scenes from myths and legends.

Stop gawking like a country bumpkin, Ada snapped *at herself.*

She stared hard at her father's back as they passed up the stairs and along a grand hallway. *Why did you make me stay isolated in Ilnora all those years? Did you want me to feel inadequate when today finally came or did you simply forget about me?*

All the while Rishard had been keeping up a murmured commentary: "– and down that corridor are the feasting chambers and beyond them the indoor water-gardens, but we're heading to the Great Hall – a bit of a misnomer really, it is tiny by comparison. It was the old throne room in the original castle before mad King Josét made all the grand extensions (and now no-one knows whether to call this Vière Castle or the Vière Palace). But if there is anything ceremonial to be done, it's done in the Great Hall."

Lord Dura turned and gave him a look, silently ordering silence. Rishard obeyed.

"Who seeks to enter His Majesty's court?"

They had reached the Great Hall.

Her father, Fillipe and Callum all gave the ceremonial responses but Ada was no longer listening.

I'm about to meet the king. Her throat felt dry and her right temple began to throb again.

Dura caught Ada's eye and gave her a rare, encouraging look. She tried to smile in return but only managed an awkward grimace.

She wished she had spent the carriage journey revising what she was supposed to do. She began to mentally rehearse the ceremony, but too late. The guards parted, and they all moved forward.

Murmurs and rustlings filled the air. Ada could sense the courtiers examining her and Rishard as they advanced towards the throne. She tried to ignore them. A wooden throne, intricately carved and inlaid with gold, sat on a raised dais against a drapery of luscious colours. A figure in a sky-blue doublet stood up from the throne but Ada didn't look at him directly. It was only as they reached the foot of the dais that she let her eyes flit upwards. She was shocked to see how much grey flecked the king's nut-brown hair and how darkly lined his forehead was. He was only thirty-two.

His Majesty caught her staring and flashed her the ghost of a wink.

6

The King and the Stone

Ada looked down, as if bowing her head in respect.

The king had winked at her – the king. What would people think? Had anyone seen it? Had her father? How were you meant to behave with a king who winked at you in public? The absurdity of it suddenly struck her: the king had winked at her. Wrestling a spasm of laughter that threatened to undo her decorum, she thereafter avoided eye contact with the king and let Rishard lead her through the motions of the ceremony. Everything went smoothly.

Finally, the king joined their extended hands as a sign of his approval and proclaimed: "The betrothal of Count Rishard il Frénore and the Lady Ada il Dura is hereby recognised by my court."

King Rencival indicated for them to rise and, without waiting for the solemn atmosphere to dissipate, began to talk.

"It is now your privilege to be introduced to my entire council. By the end you'll be wishing you were one of the lower nobility, who are spared this rigmarole. But should you survive the ordeal you'll be my honoured guests at the Assembly of Artisans afterwards."

A quiver of delight shot up Ada's spine. She thought she would never be allowed to go to the Assembly of Artisans. King Rencival had established it five years ago, inviting the most skilled craftsman in Aven to display their goods before the court. The reports of beauty and grandeur had made Ada ache with longing. Now at last, she was going to see it for herself.

But not quite yet. As His Majesty had promised, they first had to be introduced to each individual member of the council and, as His Majesty had also promised, it was horribly tedious. As Rishard later pointed out, they would usually have just met the few officials who advised the king all year round but, partly because of the summer events at court and partly because of the pending visit of the ambassadors from Nordlann, the full council of magnates were present.

At first, Ada was grateful for having proper introductions and the chance to learn who was who. (Although the line of nobles began with Baron Ashilda, who kissed her hand with a knowing smile. Ada wiped it clean on the back of her dress.) Yet after meeting the Chancellor Elkron, the Lords Velderan, Kishere, Rothford and countless others, she began to feel dizzy. Of course, these weren't their real names but their titles which went with the land they had inherited or had been given to them by the king. Her own family name, Dura, was derived from a small valley in the south of Aven. Ironic, when one considered that her father's lands now covered nearly a third of the entire country.

"I hear," said Rencival to Dura, as they ended the line of introductions, "that I have to congratulate you on a spectacular ball last night. I was desperate to come, but Elkron insisted that it would be against tradition. He had to summon half a dozen guards to hold me down. But Ashilda here gave me a very vivid description of the event."

"Your Highness is too kind," Dura replied, ignoring Ashilda who had stepped forward to bow at the mention of his name. "I am only sorry that tradition compelled your absence."

"Yes, traditions do have their downsides."

"Speaking of which," interrupted a lady who had been standing behind Rishard, "it is high time we were proceeding with events."

The king inclined his head to her before turning back to Ada and Rishard. "I have the honour of one last introduction, one I should have started with."

"Yes, you should have." The lady narrowed her twinkling eyes in jesting accusation, a mannerism strongly reminiscent of Meruda. Ada felt an instant liking to her.

Unperturbed, Rencival continued. "Rishard and Ada, may I present the Lady Elina el Rienna, my cousin. As I am yet unmarried, Elina takes it upon herself to act as the figurehead for female royalty on these occasions."

Ada curtsied. Here was someone her father had told her about. For besides Rencival himself, Elina was the only full-blooded royal alive and both were unmarried and childless, despite (or maybe because of) Lord Dura urging them to marry, produce heirs and secure the long-term stability of the kingdom. After one such failed attempt, Lord Dura had commented that Lady Elina might be the apparent soul of friendliness but would hold a grudge to the grave. For her part, Ada's sympathies lay entirely with the royals. Their struggles against her father's pressurising were akin to hers; appropriate when you considered that they were in fact distant relatives, if you went back several generations.

"Now as my cousin suggested," continued Rencival, "we had better be making our way to the Assembly. They'll be sending search parties out if we wait much longer."

"I doubt they would have the impertinence sire," said the Lord Rothford, in a tone as sour as a lemon.

Rencival's eyes glinted, whether with mischief or anger, Ada couldn't tell. "In that case," he said, "we better go quickly; we don't want to risk the commoners growing restless." With that, he took Elina's hand and led the company towards the outer courtyards where an incredible scene met their eyes.

Silverware and precious stones sparkled out from their nests of black fabric; silks flowed down over manikins, and the scent of warm pastries filled the air. There were tables laden with books; paper and quills; tapestries and dresses; sugar carvings and ale brews. Examples of carved chairs and tables spilled out into the walkway, along with display racks of weaponry and armour. There was even a horse in a fantastic array of livery, which shook its head irritably to drive the flies away, making the tiny bridle bells ring with a vengeance.

"FIGS!"

Ada jumped.

King Rencival's explosion silenced the courtyard. Everyone watched as he surged towards the nearest stall which was heavily laden with a rich variety of fruits. Rencival halted stock-still opposite the fruitier, heaving deep breaths, as if too angry for words. Then he began to bark demands with indignant savagery:

"I'm a poor man, I eat but poor fare;

So spare an old fig, the worst of your wares."

The fruitier re-joined in a sing-song voice, an enormous grin plastering his face: *"That's a shame but they're saved for the king."*

"Why? Has he no money to buy better than I?"

"Not *a fig to spend, that's him."*

They finished in unison then collapsed with laughter.

Ada felt a gentle squeeze on her arm. Glancing at Rishard, she saw him drop his jaw with a pointed air. Ada took the hint and closed her gaping mouth while Rishard shook with a soundless chuckle. It was all very well for him to laugh at her surprise, but no-one had warned her that the king liked to break into nursery rhymes.

"Elina, what are you doing? Bring Lady Ada and Count Frénore over."

His Majesty moved from stall to stall talking with each trader and craftsman with friendly camaraderie, perfectly recalling all their names and details of their businesses with astonishing detail. It was easy to spot the more established merchants as they were visibly relaxed and spoke freely, though respectfully, always letting His Majesty direct the conversations. Every now and then, Elina would cut in with a quick-witted comment that sent king and commoner into fits of laughter; a sight that made Chancellor Elkron's nose wrinkle. For he, along with all the court officials and nobility, trailed behind the king, silently watching the proceedings.

Ada wasn't quite sure what to make of it herself, especially when King Rencival tried to get them to join in with his jokes. Ada could sense the stifled disapproval radiating from their noble entourage. She wondered if Rencival could sense it, until she glimpsed the mischievous twinkle every time he turned to make innocent recommendations to his courtiers.

Eventually, after nearly an hour (and a small cough from the Chancellor), His Majesty sighed and turned to address the nobles. "Very well, you've waited long enough. Disperse and order your own household furnishings."

As one, the group bowed and dispersed. All except Dura who stepped forward. "Then, if it pleases Your Majesty, I will excuse myself."

"Oh." Rencival sounded genuinely disappointed. "I thought you enjoyed this kind of thing."

Ada could hardly believe her ears. It was difficult to imagine her father enjoying anything, let alone this.

Her father inclined his head. "All the same there are things –"

"There are more important things you need to do, yes, yes, don't waste your breath. If you need to go, you need to go, but I expect you to wait on me even earlier tomorrow morning."

"As Your Majesty commands." Dura bowed, kissed Elina's hand and Ada's forehead, nodded to Rishard and strode away.

"He has a way of doing things, your father," Rencival sighed. "Now you two, off you go and enjoy yourselves. Ada has my royal permission to spend all her father's money."

Off they went, but it wasn't long before they had separated: Rishard being engrossed at an exhibition of armoury whilst Ada wandered idly on.

She passed a long trestle table that was laden with wide, shallow dishes piled high with coloured powders. Ada stepped closer to smell the spices then wished she hadn't: they clogged the air with a riot of rich aromas that made her choke and her eyes sting. Ada hurried away to a quiet corner, trying to hide her streaming eyes.

When she could see clearly again, she realised she was next to the mirrorstone stall. She glanced at the amused stallholder who had watched the whole eye-watering incident. Ada gave him a sheepish smile and buried herself in the mirrorstone display.

She loved mirrorstone. It was a very common crystalline rock, but when treated with irilda oil the crystal could absorb and faintly emit light. The more irilda oil was used, the brighter the stone would glow. Of course, as irildas were more expensive than gold, making such an ornament cost a small fortune. You could still get exquisite trinkets and carvings with the untreated mirrorstone, it just wasn't as special. Then again, this stall was for royal custom, so naturally every piece was glowing to one degree or another.

Ada was thrilled to find that they had panel-carvings, made by layering thin panes of engraved crystal and then searing them together into one block. A clever artisan could create exquisite landscapes, especially if they managed to dye the individual panes.

In pride of place reposed a leather-bound book. Curious, Ada picked it up. It was a Light Lore – a real Light Lore – the source of all their knowledge about the dragons. She had once glimpsed Guardian Rosquebelle's copy, back home in Ilnora, but she had never actually held one before, let alone read one. She opened it reverently. It was indeed made like a book, its pages glistening leaves of the crystal, so thin it was incredible they hadn't been shattered when the words had been engraved. She gingerly fingered the panes, fascinated. A loose black velvet cloth nestled behind the first one, doubtless to separate the pages when reading. It was an exquisite piece of workmanship.

The stall holder looked uncomfortable at her selection. "I'm sorry mi'lady, but I'm only really meant to sell copies of *The Light Lore* to the guardians."

"Why?"

He looked even more uncomfortable. "Well it's...it's not the done thing. Can't have people reading stuff they don't understand and then getting wrong ideas."

She laughed. "I'm hardly going to get ideas. I am not a great academic student trying to prove the world wrong. I am a faithful dragelda; I just want to know more."

"Well..."

"Oh, please."

He hesitated. "Very well. For you ma'am."

Ada felt her cheeks go pink with pleasure. Only officially recognised courtiers were called ma'am. "Thank you so much."

"Ada," Rishard called, leaning from around the stall, "come and see the acrobats, they're just starting."

"Just a moment." Ada quickly told the man to charge it to the Dura account and he assured her he would deliver the package by evening.

Satisfied, Ada let Rishard lead her away.

7

Up in Smoke

Acrobats bounced and whirled; musicians strummed and tooted until they were red in the face and the crowd applauded. Ada's cheeks ached with laughing and smiling, but still her eyelids kept drooping down. Sleep was trying to catch up with her. She tried to force her eyes open to watch the entertainers. A piece of red cloth tied to a dancer's waist spun round and round...

A slight nudge prodded her into wakefulness. Beside her Rishard was cheering and clapping the bowing acrobats. He elbowed her again. Ada hastily joined in the applause.

"Good, weren't they?" Rishard murmured.

"Thank you," she breathed back.

"Waking you is apparently my main role today...Just promise me next time you won't snore."

"You, sir, are rude."

"At least I don't snore."

She kicked him. Discreetly. After all, they were in public. In public. She bit her lip. "Um, Rishard, how long was I...?"

"Only a matter of moments. Don't worry, I think you did a remarkable job of staying upright. And we're in an alcove, no-one saw."

Ada scanned the rows of courtiers seated on the stone shelves lining the sunken stage, careful to maintain her façade of a smile. Rishard was probably right.

She caught sight of a face in the crowd looking at her, a man's face, one she was sure she recognised. She looked closer, but he was gone. Ada blinked. How could he have just disappeared? She studied that area of the spectators again but to no avail. Was she imagining things? Had her abduction made her paranoid or was someone watching her?

Her scanning eye was drawn to the preparations for the next act. A crowd of servants were ferrying shallow stone troughs, full of brightly glowing coals, and arranging them in two concentric circles under the direction of an old man. Once in position, two younger men started moving from one stone trench to another, sprinkling in dyes that would colour and thicken the smoke. These two wore leather baldrics strapped across their chests, from which hung the strangest collection of small metal pipes.

Ada's eyes gleamed. They were Smoke Charmers, storytellers who manipulated smoke to give imagery to their tales. The older man must be the narrator, the two youngsters his apprentices who would coax the smoke into meaningful shapes using their hands and blow-pipes.

As the dye burnt, coloured smoke built up over the individual trenches. The patches of colour hung low over the coals, too heavy to rise any further, but the rich, cloying scent spread out and filled the air, the smell of a good story about to be told.

Expectancy tingled through Ada.

"What tale shall I tell my lords and ladies?" the old Smoke Charmer called. His voice creaked from years of breathing smoke, but still it reverberated with power.

Several suggestions were called out at once. The Smoke Charmer smiled at their enthusiasm. Yet he called over the heads of his seated audience, "My Lord King, which tale do you wish me to tell?"

Ada hadn't noticed the king joining the party. Nor, apparently, had anyone else for everyone quickly rose and bowed.

Rencival was leaning against a pillar at the back of the crowd, half-concealed among the leaves of a clematis as he swirled a goblet, annoyance at being noticed clearly etched on his face. His voice cracked sharp: "I have no particular inclination, old man."

"Tell us of the Infinity Isle," called Callum, Chief of the Dragnoss Guardians. He was seated off to the right, just visible to Ada as she craned her neck.

Ada hadn't liked his smile earlier and she liked it even less now: it was reminiscent of a predator preparing to pounce. Perhaps the Smoke Charmer thought so too, as she saw wary recognition flash across his face. Yet he still turned to the king for royal approval.

Rencival waved his hand. "Yes, yes - do the Infinity Isle before we die of infinite boredom. Although it's hardly an imaginative choice Callum."

Callum's smile widened under his shark eyes. "We can never hear too much of the dragons, sire."

The old man signalled to his apprentices. They exchanged glances but set to work creating the first scene, sucking in the smoke from the trenches and then puffing it out in the centre of the ring: one created a sea of blue fog whilst the other blew out great plumes of greenish-grey, which he then shaped into mountain peaks with swift, sweeping motions.

Their master stood silent for a few moments, giving the kneeling pair time to finish the base cloud. Then he began, slowly circling around the outer ring as he spoke.

"The Infinity Isle was the first home of our kind," intoned the old Smoke Charmer. "The sea surrounded it but the land had no end. You could travel for eternity and not reach the centre and yet you could reach the sea shore within a few moments just by wishing to.

"The island was beautiful with every possible landscape: cliffs...mountains...forests..."

Both apprentices were fast at work, each puffing green smoke from a blow-pipe shaped like an antler. Dark green trailed out in complex patterns from the multiple openings, but after a moment, with a quick twist of the mouthpiece, the smoke was funnelled into a single trail, emerging from one central pipe as the Smoke Charmers sank to a squat, resulting in a majestic smoke-tree, hanging mid-air. The action was repeated so rapidly as the apprentices bobbed up and down, that in no time at all a whole forest of smoke-trees had sprung up.

"There were plains, even deserts, but of a friendly kind, now unknown to us, for wherever one went there was always water available. Springs, pools and lakes to drink, dive and swim in. There was nothing missing."

Fingers whirled through a succession of small but strangely shaped pipes to form the other landscapes described. They even inhaled some of the blue smoke representing the sea and blew it out as waterfalls and rivers. The assortment of metal mouthpieces and blow pipes hanging from their clothes tinkled gently as they swung and clinked into each other, the sound rippling through the air like a wind chime in a summer breeze.

Ada leant back, letting her vision blur so that the island seemed to be floating just in front of her, bright fields of flowers swaying within her grasp.

"This was the first home of our ancestors, the only time in history when lantyns were utterly pellucid; their bodies like living diamonds with no vestige of darkness or blemish marring them. And more than this, they were filled with light. For their life and joy flowed from the Morning Star, the Living Fire who lived in the lantyns' hearts making their bodies shine gloriously bright, so that lantynkind on the Infinity Isle mirrored the stars of the night sky.

"Other creatures lived on the island, but the most spectacular were the salamanders, the great winged lizards, whose bodies were formed entirely of fire. Yet these fiery beasts could walk through a tinder-dry forest without setting it alight and swim underwater without being extinguished. Their fire was immortal because it flowed from the Morning Star.

"Yet for all that, lantyns were the only beings who could have the Morning Star living *within* them.

"Every evening the salamanders would join our ancestors by the pools and the lakes and together they would sing. The music would cause the irildas at the bottom of the lakes to blossom, their flames unaffected by the water. The open irildas would rise to the water's surface and drift up into the sky, filling it with fresh stars every night.

"It was a land and time of perfect balance.

"Yet whilst lantyns could swim without fear in the water of the pools and lakes, they were warned that the water of the sea would bring darkness to their hearts."

It's all a little inevitable, thought Ada. *Whenever there's a condition to happiness it's all bound to go wrong*. She knew the story – who didn't? One day their ancestors ignored the warning and swam in the sea, the fire left their hearts and the sea swept them away from the Infinity Isle into the Grey Realm. The dragons (whom the Smoke Charmer had mistakenly called salamanders) wanted to help the lost lantyns, but their bodies of naked flame would only cause destruction in the Grey Realm, so they coated themselves with the pebbles of the Infinity Isle, a scaly coat to contain their fire. Then they came to the Grey Realm to breathe fire back into lantyns' hearts.

Another sudden surge of sleepiness washed through her. Ada sat up straighter, but it wasn't enough. Her eyelids drooped. The Smoke Charmer's sonorous voice was soothing and soon was only an indistinct flow of sound, drifting over her head...

"...so the lantyns listened to the dragon and went into the sea."

What? Ada's eyes jolted open. A dragon persuaded the lantyns to go into the sea? That wasn't how the story went. As she glanced around, Ada realised that she hadn't misheard. Unrest stirred. Most of the listeners were already leaving amid a buzz of scandalised murmuring. Ada wondered how long the discontent had been building. She kicked herself for not listening and focused on the Smoke Charmer. Rishard was plucking at her arm, but Ada was too interested in trying to catch up with the story.

The Smoke Charmer was speaking louder so as to be heard over the shuffling movement. "The sea sucked under their feet and whirled into a giant waterspout surrounding the Island's shore before it came crashing down to spew the lantyns out and away until they were washed up on the shores of the Grey Realm." He picked up speed and volume as he saw his audience disperse and the royal guardsmen advance. The two apprentices had long stopped shaping the smoke.

"*Ada!*" urged Rishard in an undertone, this time gripping her arm.

She yielded and let him lead her out along with everyone else, but her ears strained behind her, trying to catch more of the Smoke Charmer's tale.

"Their hearts, and the hearts of their children ever after, were poisoned with darkness. Thus, the dragons triumphed, enslaving people in their night –"

They were passing through the doorway. Ada looked back. Several guards were surrounding the Smoke Charmer, ordering silence. Still, the Smoke Charmer's voice boomed out.

"The only promise of light we can trust is that of the Morning Star!"

Rishard tugged her into the sunshine. The oak doors slammed shut behind them.

The rest of the day rolled by. King Rencival oversaw the various amusements with his usual jovial manner, but it wasn't enough to allay Ada's unease. Unlike earlier, Rishard remained by her side attentive, too attentive for comfort. She could sense a storm brewing behind his polite manners and dreaded the moment when it would break.

Eventually, Rencival gave them leave to go and they found themselves cloistered in the carriage again.

"What were you thinking?" Rishard burst out as they drove away.

"What do you mean?"

"Why did you try to stay and listen to that Smoke Charmer?"

"I had fallen asleep and was confused as I woke: I couldn't believe he was making the dragons the villain. I was making sure I hadn't misunderstood."

"*Ada, dear,*" Rishard said, as if talking to a little child. "Being fair-minded is all very well, but it's dangerous to be seen doing anything that could be thought of as unpatriotic, and listening to anything that slanders dragons is most definitely unpatriotic. That Smoke Charmer was probably a Burning Heart and by lingering to listen you risk getting us tarred with the same brush."

Ada winced. All her life she had heard whispers of Burning Hearts. The stories varied hugely; depicting anything from vicious maniacs to docile idiots, but it was well known that Burning Hearts believed some disturbing notions about dragons. She remembered how Callum had eyed the old Smoke Charmer before he had even begun his tale: Callum had known or suspected.

"Conformity is essential," Rishard went on. "Our survival depends on it. Last year, the court of Errivel tore itself apart from the inside: now they are the latest vassal of the Nordish Empire. Why do you think everyone's on tenterhooks with the coming delegation from Nordlann? Especially when you consider that they've been making frequent incursions on our northern borders but their stated purpose in coming is to discuss the nard trade! Do you see? They're sizing us up. We need to be careful. *You* need to be careful."

Ada grimaced and gave a single nod. It was galling to admit it, but she ought to have known better than to publicly indulge her naïve curiosity. Yet how could Rishard speak to her like that? So condescending and superior. He sounded just like her father. Being right only worsened his crime. But how was she meant to know about political intricacies when she had been kept in the far south all her life? Her knowledge of the wider world relied on quizzing the odd travelling merchant, when and if she had been allowed to see any. Ada curled her fingers into a tight fist, resentment simmering.

They trundled on in silence.

It was only as they reached the Dura mansion that Rishard spoke again.

"That blacksmith had some fascinating ideas about interlacing chainmail. I wonder if he would consider coming south for a while to lick my man into shape."

Ada murmured assent but inwardly seethed. How could he be thinking about his silly armoury already? He had made her feel totally ignorant, small and worthless, and the first thing he chose to talk about was chainmail!

Rishard didn't seem to read her thinly-veiled resentment as he said a cheery farewell. The moment he was out of sight her smile dropped. She wheeled around, marched to her room and began to pace, hands clenching and unclenching, feeling desperate to do something to release her restless energy. Would she never be free from lectures and scolding; forever trapped under someone else's dictates; condemned for ignorance others had fostered? She wanted to hurl something at a wall, but smashing things would only bring more trouble.

Maybe a bath would help me cool down.

She turned to give the order to Meruda and suddenly realised that Meruda was not there. In fact, now she thought about it, Meruda hadn't even been in the carriage on the way back from the castle. She ought to have been ready and waiting to accompany them. Where had she got to? She had probably wandered off, missed their return and was now having to walk back by herself. Oh well, Meruda could look after herself and somebody else would get the bath started. Ada rang the bell and threw herself in a chair.

There was a knock at the door.

"Come in," Ada called, loosening her hair in preparation.

To her surprise it was Kessler who entered, although he was followed by one of the maidservants. She was young, although probably a few years older than Ada, and slightly built but would have stood taller if not for the diffident hunch of her shoulders. Her hair, a mousey-brown colour, was tied loosely back under a serving cap, revealing a delicate oval face, although her glass skin was unfortunately pockmarked over the cheek bones. For a moment her golden-grey eyes locked with Ada's amber-green in mutual curiosity, before the girl lowered her gaze.

Probably a new house maid Kessler wants me to be kind to.

Kessler had a habit of wanting Ada to do nice things that he said befitted the lady of the house. That had all been very well when she had been a little girl, but now she was the lady of the house and he was the steward. She might not be of age, but her marriage had been arranged and the king had received her at court; Kessler really couldn't keep doing this. She would have to speak to him when they were alone, yet for now she would be civil.

"What can I do for you?" she asked.

Kessler bowed. "My lady, I am sorry to tell you this, but Meruda is no longer employed in this household's service."

Ada laughed. “Don’t be ridiculous Kessler. She might have missed the carriage, but I wouldn’t send her away for it.”

“This is not about her leaving you unchaperoned with your fiancé, although that would have been cause enough for dismissal.”

“Then out with it: what’s her crime? Stolen another pastry from the cook? Whatever it is, I am sure you can sort it out. Besides, I wouldn’t have another maid for worlds – Meruda’s irreplaceable. Now go and tell her to prepare a bath for me.”

“Please, my lady.” His tone made her look at him again. He was serious. “She was caught trying to break into your father’s strongroom.”

“What?” She snorted in disbelief. “Meruda? I don’t believe it. There must be some misunderstanding. Let’s hear what she has to say.”

“She’s gone, my lady.”

Fear suddenly clutched at Ada’s stomach as she thought of the penalties for stealing. Surely not. Her father wouldn’t…

“She ran away,” Kessler’s voice cut through her thoughts. “Your father’s men were sent to hunt her down but they haven’t come back yet. Lord Dura commissioned me to find you a replacement maid and I have chosen Iris.”

Ada felt adrift. Meruda gone for good and without goodbye and instead she was left with…Ada’s gaze fell on the girl in front of her. Her eyes narrowed. “I assume you are Iris?”

The girl bowed and nodded in one flinching motion.

Ada turned to Kessler. “I must compliment you,” she said in biting tones, “on how fast you found a replacement maid when the old one was scarcely out of the door. Tell me, how long have you and my father been planning this between you?"

Kessler began to reply but Ada didn't wait. She stormed out, heading towards her father's study.

Meruda a thief? Preposterous. It was more likely that her father had suddenly decided that he did not approve of Meruda's friendship and wanted to get rid of her. That was why he had left court so early, so that he could arrange this. But why did he have to make Kessler part of it? Somehow that made everything ten times worse. Kessler had never lied to her before and she never thought he would, even if ordered to.

Seething with hurt and betrayal, she reached her father's study and faltered, suddenly unsure. Then Meruda's face swam into her mind, and she stepped forward, raised her hand to knock and stopped, hand frozen in mid-air. She could already hear his denial and crushing rebuke. It wouldn't do any good. It would only make things worse.

Resolve shattered. Ada lowered her hand and walked away.

8

Over the Border

Kelvin ran as he never had before.

The short sharp blasts from the brassnet horns chased him down the valley like a pack of baying hounds. The hunt was nearly up.

Terror gave him wings and he all but flew over bog and scrub. Orla bounced up and down in his arms, her tiny fingers clasped tight around the back of his neck. Her hair blew loose and wild, the odd strand catching in Kelvin's mouth. He puffed them out as he ploughed onwards, heading towards the clump of trees that clustered around a fold in the mountainside. Dusk was fast approaching. If only they could get down to that line of trees, they might be able to hide.

Angry desperation surged through him. It was all so unfair. They weren't in Nordlann anymore. They had passed the border-stone – they were in Aven. Had they spent weeks of skirting and dodging patrols only to get arrested when they were meant to be safe?

He rounded a jutting cliff. Dark shapes loomed ahead: houses. Kelvin swerved away to the left, towards the trees. He couldn't risk the village being unfriendly to strangers, let alone fugitives.

The brassnet sounded again, much nearer than last time and now he could hear orders being shouted.

Kelvin charged on, panic driving him forwards. Orla's thin, starved form weighed heavy in his arms now. His lungs were burning. Each pounding footfall jarred up his spine. Why was he so slow? Faster. Faster. He pushed his protesting legs on.

A faint roaring grew ahead. It was a continuous sound and growing louder. A river? Too late. One foot had already stepped over the brink. His limbs flailed in the air, vainly trying to regain his footing. They fell, tumbling down a steep descent. Orla gave a brief scream and then they crash-landed at the bottom. A sharp rock struck the top of Kelvin's right shin, just below the knee, igniting a fireball of pain. For a moment he was unable to move except to curl up in agony.

Orla gave a terrified whimper. "Kelvy?"

Kelvin heaved himself up, swallowing a howl.

The light was nearly gone now, but the white fleck and foam of the river was still visible. There was nothing for it. He braced himself and plunged forward. It was icy cold, even colder than he had imagined it could be, and slippery too. His right leg kept buckling under his weight and the buffeting current. He stumbled. Orla shrieked as she was half-dunked. Kelvin held her as high out of the water as he could. Her fingers dug into his skin in panic. Gasping through his clenched teeth, eyes watering with hot tears, Kelvin ploughed on.

The river was not wide or particularly deep, but by the time he floundered onto the gravel bank opposite, they were both soaked and chilled to the bone.

Above the churning river the brassnet rang.

With a faint groan, Kelvin dragged himself and Orla behind a rock. He curled himself up as small as possible, hugging the teeth-chattering Orla. He had no more time or strength to do anything else.

The moments passed.

As they were not immediately seized and hauled out from their hiding place, Kelvin began to listen. A confused medley of thumping hooves and shouts rose above the rushing water and rustling breeze. It continued for some time. Gradually the hullabaloo quietened down to a single strand of noise, just audible above the water, with odd parts snatched away by the wind.

Kelvin strained his ears.

The voices were raised, half-shouting in argument, and they were speaking in Avenese, not Nordish. He listened hard, suddenly thankful for all those years of study he endured.

The first voice belonged to an Avenese native, but the second to his old master, the Lord Saupa. It was unmistakable.

Saupa himself?

Kelvin's heart pounded. Saupa was hunting him in person. Of course he was: laying aside his personal grievance, he couldn't risk Kelvin warning Dura. Kelvin racked his brains, trying to remember the date but he had hopelessly lost track of time when crossing the mountains. Not that it mattered, for if Saupa was here then that farce of an ambassadorial visit couldn't have happened yet. He still might be able to get to Dura in time...

The native was talking again. "An' I don't care who ye are, ye can clear out – yur racket is scaring the sheep no end."

"And I am telling you that I have a man down there, a fugitive from the law. Now will you help me get him out or not?"

"In case ye missed the border-stone sir, this is Meadstone and yur in Aven now, and any man-hunting that's to be done, should be done and is done by mi'Lord Elkron. This is his land yur straying on, ye know. Ye best take the matter up with him, 'cept he's down in Casida. Ye could try Sir Endric; his manor is close by."

"I know, I came from there. But if I delay, I'll lose my man, now tell me: how do we get down there?"

"Only by jumping and I don't think ye want to do that sir. It's a fearful deep plunge."

"So, he's dead?"

"Unless ye believe in miracles."

Saupa's voice spoke again in lowered tones, but after a moment more, he raised his voice, reverting to Nordish as he ordered his men to move downriver.

Kelvin didn't trust himself to move although he wasn't sure he could now, even if he tried. So he waited, and waited, listening so intently that his head began to ache from the effort. Time and time again he thought he heard Saupa's men returning, but it was only ever the rush and rumble of the river. After each false alarm a new wave of exhaustion would crash down on him, dragging him nearer oblivion as delicious drowsiness pulled at his senses. His resistance would totter until some slight or imagined noise jolted him awake. Yet the call of sleep grew ever harder to shake off.

He was teetering on the brink of total unconsciousness when a hand clasped him on the shoulder.

Kelvin started, hitting his head on the rock. He blinked up in the flickering torchlight.

A group of kindly weather-beaten faces peered down at him. One of them was saying something, but Kelvin's mind was too numb to take any more in, especially in a foreign language. Then he felt Orla being lifted out of his grip.

Kelvin let out a strangled cry and pulled her close.

The nearest man started to speak soothingly. In one last effort, Kelvin focused on the words, trying to understand. He caught the word "safe" several times, but that was all he could manage. His grip on Orla loosened and Kelvin found himself being taken away, half-led and half-carried.

Disjointed sensations and images flitted through his mind. Stumbling over rocks...a flow of coaxing but unintelligible words...slipping and being caught, held fast in a firm but reassuring grip...being laid down on something soft...

Warmth.

Darkness.

Sleep.

Slowly, very slowly, Kelvin's mind emerged from comfortable nothingness.

He was warm, covered by a comforting weight. An intermittent crackle told him of a fire nearby, yet it wasn't bright enough to penetrate his heavy eyelids.

Different voices wove in and out of each other in a gentle web of sound.

He moved a little, trying to find a position he could hear better in, but he only created a loud rustling in his ear. He turned the movement into a sleeping stretch, such as he had seen Orla make, and settled into stillness once more, eyes shut, breathing deep and even. A few scratchy straws poked into his cheek.

"I don't care. I don't like the look of him."

Kelvin fought the instinct to stiffen. This voice was nearby and was speaking in Nordish.

"Don't be silly Tarran," a girl answered, also in Nordish. "Look at the state he's in and the chick, poor little goldenhead. Or are you going to tell me she's part of the conspiracy?"

A disgruntled *harrumph* was the only reply.

"You know I'm right. They're exiles like us and need our help."

"Stop pretending to be better than everyone," he spoke harshly. "The girl might be all right. She would be hunted down with hair like that, but he isn't. Look at him, under the dirt and rags he's all soft. Just look at those soft, soft hands, no calluses on them. Bet he's never done a real day's work in his life. You honestly think he's one of us?"

"Why not? Rank makes no difference."

"I told you to drop the cushie act. And rank does make all the difference. They wouldn't dream of killing one of their own on the spot just because someone got jealous and accused them of dragon treachery. They wouldn't cut them down in the street before they had a chance to speak."

"Tarran don't torture yourself with that..."

But Tarran carried on, "*They* would 'make enquiries' until they proved the accusation false or found a loophole. And he's one of them. Didn't you hear what they said earlier? Old Burning Eyes is here, sniffing around, looking for him. Yes, *Saupa*. Here in Aven. Now do you understand? Since when did one measly farm boy warrant the great Lord Saupa's attention? Something's up and we need to watch it. Come away now. I bet the wretch is only pretending to be asleep."

As this was the truth of the matter, Kelvin felt even more self-conscious. He ran a mental checklist over his muscles, making sure they were relaxed. He focused on keeping each breath slow and steady: in...out...in...out...

Kelvin found that he was waking up again.

For a moment he was disorientated.

He hadn't even felt himself drifting off: he had simply fallen asleep and, just as suddenly, he had emerged from it to full wakefulness. It was the first time in an age that he had slept properly, and he felt it. Instead of aching, his limbs felt light and buzzing with the urge to get up and investigate. He sat up.

Orla lay at his feet, resembling a contented cat as she sprawled out on her back, her hands peeping out from under the thick blankets to just touch her ears, a happy smile on her face. Her golden hair glinted among the straw.

He stared, once more struck by her sheer tranquillity. How could she look so peaceful, even in sleep? She had been scared enough last night, but that was gone now and she slept as she always did: deep and peacefully without a lingering trace of terror. It grated Kelvin that she never had nightmares. It seemed unnatural.

Why does that upset you? Do you want her to be terrified all the time like you?

Ashamed, he pushed the little voice away and looked around.

He and Orla were lying on a bed of straw at the end of a single-roomed hut. It was not a particularly large room, judging by the grey light which was peeping through tiny holes in the stone walls and the shutters, but it was full of people. Most were still lying asleep on the floor, but some were rising and getting ready for another day.

Someone spotted that Kelvin was awake, smiled and picked his way through the sleepers to reach Kelvin's side. It was the weather-beaten face that smiled on him last night and told him he was safe. Kelvin wondered if he was the same shepherd who had misdirected Saupa.

"All right, lad?" he asked in Avenese.

His manner was friendly enough but Kelvin's mouth had gone dry. What should he say? These peasants might be welcoming. They had protected him from Saupa, but that other man, Tarran, was another matter. He sounded like he was ready for revenge and Kelvin was a very suitable scapegoat.

As his thoughts whirled, the man frowned.

"Nay lad, don't be frightened," he said. "It's a touch tricky I'll admit when ye don't understand me. My face is hardly a sight to wake up to. Ach, where's that Tarran when ye want him."

"He's gone to the higher fields," grunted one of the figures on the floor. "Out of the way of that there Nordlann laird."

The man bit his lip and paused. "It's probably best that that hothead is out of the way. But for now..." He turned his eyes back on Kelvin. "Let me see...er...ah yes! Vee-schull... er...Vee-schull metz. Ye be safe here, lad."

Kelvin smiled. It wasn't a bad attempt at Nordish. Of course, he understood every word the man was saying in Avenese, now his brain wasn't dog-tired, but he kept quiet. It would be better to feign ignorance for now.

"There now," the shepherd clapped his hands at Kelvin's smile. "That's better. Now, let us see about getting ye breakfast."

As he spoke, the door opened: women and girls came in chattering. They put down their various baskets and jars and busily started preparing food. Those still lying down were unceremoniously chivvied awake and up.

The old shepherd called towards the newcomers. "Yanita."

One of the girls put down her bucket and came over. As she approached it became clear that she wasn't a girl but a young woman. Her dainty frame was obscured by a gloriously thick fuzziness of reddish-brown hair which fell down to her waist. She caught Kelvin's eye and gave a shy smile, the corners of her large brown eyes crinkling with a merry, welcoming warmth.

Kelvin stared, captivated. Under the merry twinkle he recognised the lurking shadow of sadness, which echoed the ache in his own heart. She knew something of his pain; those kind, sincere eyes told him she understood. She drew him in. But he could also sense that she didn't want to draw him in. She simply wished him well, genuinely wished it, but she radiated a peace that was already complete and independent from him.

"It's good to see ye lass," the shepherd said. "Could you...?" He gestured to Kelvin.

"Welcome to Aven," she said to Kelvin in Nordish. "The people here are very kind, but we must not put them at risk. You know that Saupa," she winced as she said the name, "has no qualms about the lengths he will go to. He doesn't recognise the borders where the dragons' honour is concerned."

Kelvin nodded.

Yanita glanced at Orla, who, despite the noise, was still sleeping. The gentleness in her eyes deepened. "He was after the child?"

Remembering Tarran, Kelvin decided to try to knock some polish off his accent and sound a bit rougher. "Her mother asked me to take her to family in Aven. But Saupa was already chasing me. I...served him once but, well, things changed. I changed and I had to run." He looked sidelong at Yanita. Despite his admission, her face was all sympathy. His heart rose.

"Her poor mother. Is she...?"

Kelvin nodded. "With Yhari, along with her father and brothers." He referenced Yhari on an impulse and his guess was rewarded with an even sweeter, sadder smile. Yanita leant forward, clearly longing to sweep Orla up into her arms.

"So is the lad ready for breakfast?" They both jumped when the shepherd spoke. He had waited so patiently, despite not understanding a word, that they had forgotten he was there.

"I thinking he wanting breakfast," Yanita replied in Avenese.

Kelvin bit his lip, restraining the urge to correct her. You don't know any Avenese, he told himself.

"Please," he said in Nordish. They both paused to look at him. "Thank you for your kindness but Orla and I must go. Saupa will come again to look for us and he'll find you," Kelvin nodded at Yanita. "He'll hurt you for helping us and tricking him." He gestured at the shepherd and the whole hut in general.

At a questioning glance from the shepherd, Yanita quickly translated.

The shepherd nodded as he muttered to himself. "'Tis all too true. Them Nordlannders keep coming, pushing the bounds of their authority and Sir Endric's not always on hand." He looked up at Kelvin. "And where would ye go lad?"

Kelvin waited for Yanita's relay.

"To Lord Dura. Orla has family serving in his household. Her mother asked me to find them. Please, how do I find them?"

At the mention of Dura, the shepherd's grey scrubby eyebrows rose. When Yanita interpreted, he gave a low whistle.

"Well, if ye manage to get in with that laird's house lad ye'll be nicely set up for life. But lad, Laird Dura's land is in the far south."

"But Laird Dura will be in Casida now," interjected a woman who had evidently been listening for some time as she busied herself around the fireplace. "Same as Laird Elkron. All the great lairds have been summoned for a great council, or so my Marianne at the manor tells me. Laird Elkron has put off his summer visit because of it and has summoned all manner of odds and ends to be sent down. Sir Endric is going down with some of his men to guard them along the way. They'll need protection, those roads are not as safe as they could be and a heavily loaded wagon is an invitation to any brigand. In fact, my Marianne said that the wagons were so full that she doubts the master intends to live here anymore."

"What is this wagons?" Yanita asked, but the shepherd clapped his hands again.

"Of course!" he crowed. "They could ride down in the wagons – Old Gnasher won't mind. He and Frionne can keep an eye on them and help them find where Laird Dura is staying in Casida. But what time will the wagons be leaving?"

"'Bout now, I'd expect. Marianne said first light."

All was haste and movement. Kelvin was bustled up, Orla was seized (she took the whole thing very well, blinking sleepily with a grumpy pout, before snuggling against his shoulder), food was thrust into his arms and they were rushed out.

Kelvin looked back. He caught sight of Yanita, standing still and watching with confusion and a touch of regret: it had all happened too fast for her to follow the meaning. "Thank you," he called.

She smiled once more and then he lost sight of her.

9

Back to Dragnoss

"We are going to the dragnoss," Ada announced as Iris, the new maid, was doing her hair.

Surprise flitted across Iris's face but she did not speak.

"What is it?" snapped Ada. Her new maid never said anything, she just looked. Meruda had sparkled and chatted, but getting an opinion out of Iris was like dragging a millstone through mud.

Iris hesitated but seeing Ada's glare she shook her head, which only irritated Ada further.

"Don't do that. Tell me what's bothering you."

The girl swallowed. Her lips squirmed as if she were chewing over her words before speaking. "Forgive me, my lady, but I thought you had already completed the ceremonies required at the dragnoss."

"I had. This is a personal visit: I want to consult the Oracle."

Iris went white. "My lady, it's not safe."

"Don't be ridiculous."

Iris's mouth shut smartly and the girl retreated into herself. She finished arranging Ada's hair in cowed silence.

Ada sighed. Despite his most energetic efforts, her father had not found Meruda and whilst Ada was relieved for Meruda's sake, she could not help feeling more and more sorry for herself with each passing day: Iris was timid, fussing and dull. Where had Kessler picked her up from?

After three days of patient endurance, Ada had gone to the household chamberlain, demanding that he find a replacement maid. Unfortunately, Kessler had happened upon them and assumed command of the situation. After listening to Ada's complaint, he quietly said that she did not have sufficient reason to dismiss the maid. He added that she should allow time for Iris to adjust. Ada had stiffly thanked him for his advice and left, burning with indignation. For Kessler to refuse her orders in front of another servant was too humiliating for words. It showed that despite recent changes, she had as much power over the household (and anything else for that matter) as she had when a toddler. Why was Kessler still in Casida? Surely he should have returned south to resume his real duties over the Ilnora estate. What was her father thinking?

This last week had been nothing but frustration: first Meruda had disappeared and then Rishard was too occupied with business to spend any time with her or, it seemed, to keep his promise about investigating the attack on her, and until that was cleared up, Ada felt uneasy about exploring Casida. There had been nothing to do and no-one to talk to – hardly the social gaiety of court life she had expected. Yet she was the only daughter of the house of Dura. She ought to be receiving all sorts of invitations. Her father must be refusing any and all of them on her behalf without even telling her. It would be like him. He was doubtless scared that she would destroy the delicate balance of power. Even if that were so, how could she learn to wield power or do anything important if she never saw anyone important?

Was this all she would ever be: a mere toy or puppet for other people's amusement or control? She knew she was meant for more.

She wondered if things would be different if her mother were still alive. Of course they would be, but there was no point speculating over the impossible.

Her restlessness had blossomed into an idea: she would go to the Oracle. The Oracle would have answers about her destiny, maybe even about her would-be kidnappers. As the dragons' mouthpiece it was quite proper, even zealous, to seek the Oracle's guidance for your life. A thrill shot through her. The Oracle's very existence was shrouded by superstitious rumours and only the highest echelons of society (those who could pay) were allowed to visit the Oracle. Ada had a niggling suspicion that her father would not approve. That settled it: she would go.

Unfortunately, Iris would have to come too. Respectability demanded that she be chaperoned and after her fiasco with the Smoke Charmer, Ada wasn't going to risk societal disapproval again so soon.

All went smoothly: her father had left early for the palace and Kessler was busy somewhere in the gardens. They hurried down and she ordered the other carriage out for herself. The servants were surprised, but they obeyed. With no countermanding authority, what else could they do?

Ada could hardly sit still in the carriage for excitement (despite the dampening presence of Iris). All the same, she kept glancing through the window, afraid of her father's sudden appearance and command to stop, but no such mishap occurred.

Once at the dragnoss, Ada paid an exorbitant price for a handful of dried irilda petals, indicating her wish to speak to the Oracle. The hairs on the back of her neck prickled as she sensed the guardians turn to watch her. Being late morning, the atrium was relatively empty: they could all see her clearly.

Feeling conspicuous, Ada stepped up to the chasm's lip. Her feet tingled at the dizzying depths. With calm composure (or at least the appearance of it) she held her arm out straight and released a string of moon pearls she had brought, along with the irilda petals. She watched until the pearls' pale gleam and the petal's fluttering dance were swallowed by the void.

"My lady, the Oracle has sent for you." A guardian stood by her elbow.

"Thank you." Ada turned to call Iris but found that the girl was already at her side, head bent down, looking terrified.

"Aren't you going to offer your gift?" Ada asked sharply.

Iris shook her bowed head.

Trying to hide her own angry embarrassment, Ada turned back to the guardian who was gazing very sternly at Iris.

“Forgive me sir, I made so much haste in getting here that I left my maid no time to prepare a gift for herself. I beg your pardon.”

“A few coins would have sufficed,” the guardian sniffed in disdain. “However, there is no shame in an honest mistake. The Oracle is waiting for you my lady, but this...person will have to wait outside.” With that he swept away, expecting them to follow.

Ada shot a furious glare at her maid. Anger boiled up. *Meruda would never have been so forgetful. I've never felt so embarrassed in all my life. Iris will pay for that.* Simmering, she followed the guardian up to one of the small, private doors in the wall of the dragnoss citadel.

He opened it and stepped aside to reveal a yawning black entrance, much like the dragnoss itself. Sudden doubts jumped to Ada's mind as she peered into the blackness, but it would not do to turn back now. She drew herself up, thanked the guardian, tersely told Iris to wait outside until she returned, took a deep breath and walked in.

The door closed behind her. Night surrounded her.

Ada moved forwards, hands reaching out in front and then to the sides. She found a wall out to her left and then another to her right. It was a corridor which, from the feel of her feet, sloped downwards. After another moment she found that the passage curved around in a descending spiral. Her fingers traced the surface of either wall, running over little ridges and trenches.

Someone must have spent a lot of time carving in here. What a waste. So few must see it. They should have planned a few lampstands when they built this place.

The thought was still going through her head when Ada saw a dim red light glowing from around the next bend. She stumbled towards it in relief. A small flat candle sat in a tiny alcove in the wall. Another candle glimmered from another alcove in the opposite wall and beyond it another and another, dotting the passageway with light.

Her movement sent the flames flickering. Simultaneously, a strange redness shimmered along the passage. Ada looked more closely. Those swirling carvings filled the entire surface of the walls, floor and ceiling; the base of each carved groove glistened red.

As if the stone were bleeding from where it had been cut.

She pulled her fingers away repulsed, even though she knew the wall was bone dry.

The air grew thick with pungent incense, pressing in with suffocating strength. Ada coughed and swayed, suddenly dizzy.

Now, with those hypnotic patterns and rippling shades, the walls appeared to be formed from billowing red smoke. Ada moved forwards, putting a hand against the stone wall and focusing on its solid touch. She shook her head, trying to fight the illusion.

The wall fell away from her hand. Ada grappled in the air but found nothing to hold onto. She closed her eyes, breathing deeply, concentrating on the solid ground she could feel underfoot. Slowly she opened her eyes, looking only at the carvings nearest her feet at first, and then extending her field of vision.

The tunnel had opened up into a circular room. If anything, the illusion from the walls was stronger in here, making Ada feel like she was floating in a bubble, suspended in a swirling cloud of scarlet vapours.

Ada blinked hard, trying to dispel her light-headedness.

Her attention was drawn to a small figure crouching by the far wall, the one stationary thing she could see. Yet even it was not completely still, for its hands twirled some beads to and fro in ceaseless motion. Ada felt some of her trepidation melt away as she looked at the Oracle. She was *very* small, not at all menacing. In fact, she looked more like a guttersnipe playing with a favourite toy. Ada blinked again. The beads in the Oracle's fingers were moon pearls, her moon pearls, the ones she had dropped into the dragnoss and watched hurtle towards the realm's foundations just moments ago.

Just a coincidence. It would be impossible for –

It was then that Ada noticed the floor. All around that small, crouching figure lay pieces of gold and silver, jewels, bracelets, coins and a hundred other treasures.

Ada felt her heart quicken as she recognised a sliver dragon clasp studded with sapphires. It was the same design – no it was *the* same one – that she offered after her betrothal ceremony. There was an emerald set in a gold ring she remembered sending as tribute years ago; and innumerable piles of coins minted with the Dura crest. She looked and looked, with the growing conviction that she was seeing every piece of tribute she had ever given the dragons.

10

The Dragons' Mouth

"Well met, Ada il Dura. You are most welcome."

The voice was unlike anything Ada had ever heard. Two voices spoke at once, a young girl's and a deep rumbling undertone.

"Thank you." Ada was apprehensive.

The Oracle looked up.

Why, she's only a child. Ada was stunned. She realised now that she had been expecting an old crone who could give voice to ancient wisdom. Instead, she saw a young face with milky white skin, framed by long golden hair that cascaded from under her hood, but the eyes were black, wide open with an unwavering, unblinking gaze.

Ada realised she was staring. "I'm sorry."

A slight smile curved the ruby-red lips. The head bowed down again. The restless fingers never stopped toying with the pearls.

"The treasure you gave us," whisper-rumbled the Oracle, "was meant to represent the treasure of your heart: love, honour, friendship...more valuable than these trinkets."

The golden head looked up. Something deep within the black eyes danced wildly, the candles sputtered in time with it.

"You have always wanted more from life: purpose, joy, fulfilment. Yet you hold back. You never give the dragons anything of real value. Love, devotion...such things do not come in drops but oceans. Your heart is closed to us. And without first opening it, you, like most lantyns, deny yourself the power and light of the dragons."

The accusation bridled. She had always paid tribute faithfully; she never doubted their existence. Yet knowing where she was, Ada bit her tongue.

The Oracle seemed to read her mind.

"You could pour a mountain of gold down the dragnoss and still fail to give the most important thing." She rose in one fluid motion and reached out her hand at Ada and growled. "Give us your heart."

Ada started back, covering her heart with her hand. It was ridiculous, stupid, she was being over-imaginative, but in this strange, dim light those outstretched fingers looked like talons ready to claw into her.

"Don't be afraid." The rumbling undertone had almost faded entirely leaving just the girl's voice, quiet and pleading. "We didn't mean to scare you, but –" she turned her palm upwards and a flame sparked up from it, "– we can't give you light unless your heart is open to receive it."

Ada's mind was spinning. She had always thought the dragons' light was just a metaphor.

"Yes and no," answered the Oracle. "Your bodies are built to hold fire – not a fire of wood or coal, but dragon fire, which is more than a physical flame. It is the warmth of love, the spark of imagination, the light of knowledge: these are immortal. Yet it is more than an intellectual or emotional empowerment. We *are* fire."

The Oracle threw her arms wide open and roared. Flames ripped out from her mouth, erupting out and rushing around the room.

Ada lost herself. She shrieked and cowered down, throwing her arms over her head.

No heat, no painful burning ensued.

She looked up. The Oracle stood above her, backed by a coiling furnace. Her words rang clear, but the tone was gentle.

"There is power in accepting this flame; power when you truly accept the dragons' fire. Remember that. So many of your kind have forgotten. Whole generations of lantyns have passed by, their understanding eroding with time, until now many think that dragon fire is a supernatural myth, when in truth there is nothing more natural than for our fire to fill your heart. You can choose differently."

The Oracle held out her hand. What had been a sapphire-studded clasp in the shape of a dragon now dangled from a chain, transformed into a necklace. The Oracle handed it to Ada.

"Wear this and remember my words. For I hold the heart and speak the words of the dragon Ishile, the servant of Levia, the mother-dragon of Aven. You will need to be strong, daughter of Aven, for your destiny is great. Our servant is coming from the north and it is your destiny to help him unite all the southern kingdoms under our wings for such a peace as has never been known from the dawn of time itself.

"But the way is dangerous: be careful of whom you trust – beware of your maid: her mind has been poisoned and she will do anything to stop you.

"So now go and find your purpose. Follow your heart. My sirens will find you in your time of need. Do not fear. You are under our protection. Did we not send rescue when you were taken into the river tunnels? We will watch over you."

The Oracle smiled, gold flames dancing within her eyes and then she sat down.

The room was a dim, reddish cave once more.

Ada knew she was dismissed. She made her way back up the spiral walk, tingling with shock, excitement and relief. Rishard could say what he liked about dragons, but she knew better. She bubbled with thoughts. She was favoured by the dragons; they had a destiny for her and would protect *her*. And the Oracle had made a prophecy about her. Ada's mind flitted back to the Oracle's words: *our servant from the north...who would it be*? The delegation from Nordlann was due in a few days. Nothing would make more sense than that the dragons' servant-from-the-north would be among the ambassadors. Besides, he or she could hardly come from anyway else, as there was nothing else northward except the vast, self-proclaimed empire of Nordlann. But it was wonderful to know that war with Nordlann *would* be averted, and averted by *her*. With the dragons' help she would bring peace to the southern kingdoms; her purpose was bigger than she had ever dreamed.

With her new eagerness to face the world, the return journey up the surreal red path seemed very short and within a few steps she had reached the door and escaped into the open air. For a second she stood still, blinking in the bright light, then she stepped forward, intending to head back towards the entrance vestibule. She suddenly realised that Iris was nowhere to be seen. She was quite alone.

"Ada, darling."

Evidently not as alone as Ada could wish, for Elina el Rienna had emerged from behind one of the thick pillars.

The elder noblewoman smiled in exuberant greeting. "I expect you're wondering where your attendant has got to. Your father packed her off and he has been prowling around ever since, trying to get you away from the Oracle. But of course, he couldn't, not without deeply offending the guardians, which he won't."

"My father is here?" Ada hoped Elina did not hear the anxiety in her voice.

"He arrived about a minute after you did. I've never seen him so...I don't know the right word. Out of control? No, no...livid? Even that isn't near the mark."

Ada's stomach curled. "Where is he now?"

"Oh, somewhere by the dragnoss, giving a tribute to appease the guardians he's ruffled. He'll be back here in a minute or two so I had better stop wasting time." She skipped forward, linked arms with Ada and lowered her voice to an earnest whisper. "I'm so glad to catch you by yourself, although I must confess, I've been waiting since I watched you go in. Your father was furious that I didn't stop you. *He* belongs to the old superstitious way of thinking.

"Anyway, what I wanted to say, dear, was that while a little interest in the dragons' ways is necessary, too much is dangerous. Oh bless your face, you haven't got a clue what I mean, have you?"

"I think I do," returned Ada.

"Don't try *not* to look stupid dear, it always has the reverse effect. Much better to admit you don't understand me and I'll happily explain myself. Your father always tells me not to speak in riddles, even when he *knows* what I mean. That's why I refused to marry him."

Ada stopped short. "He asked you –"

"Oh dear me no. I saved him the trouble by refusing before he asked. Mind you, he probably had too much sense to propose, but I thought I'd save him the temptation. After all, with Dura's power, wealth and ancestry, my rare commodity of royal blood and the fact that Rencival is unwed and childless...well, our marriage would have been very destabilising to my cousin's reign. And Dura has too much loyalty and common sense to risk that."

Ada listened to Elina's stream of words in a daze. The mere idea of Elina as her stepmother was one thing, but the resulting implications were overwhelming.

"But never mind all that," Elina said, interrupting Ada's thoughts. "The point I was making is that you showed too much interest in that Smoke Charmer's story and now this?

Sneaking off to visit the Oracle? You're taking it all far too seriously. Or at least you appear to be, which is worse."

Ada struggled to find a polite answer; Elina's revelations had fogged her faculties. "I –"

"Ada!"

She flinched. Her father stormed towards her, Callum in tow. He managed a curt bow to Elina before turning a vengeful eye on his daughter. "You have finished your consultation then?" Each syllable quivered with intensity.

"I trust," interjected Callum, in a pacifying tone, looking down at Ada, "that you have found the answers you were seeking, although I must reproach you for doing it without your father's knowledge. Your desire was good and right, but the way you went about it leaves room for improvement."

"That it does," growled Dura. "My thanks, master guardian and my lady. Now if you will excuse us." He led Ada off to the carriage. A gleam of hope returned when she saw one of their coachmen holding Dester, her father's great black riding horse, saddled and ready for mounting. Ada tried to escape, saying that she needed to look for her maid and would travel home shortly.

"I sent her walking back," he replied tersely. "I'm going to escort you home myself. One of the grooms can ride him."

He relinquished his iron grip on her arm at the door, handed her in, climbed in afterwards and threw himself into the seat beside her.

Silence.

"What were you thinking? Consulting an Oracle. Do you have any idea how dangerous that was?"

"Dangerous?" faltered Ada. "She is the mouthpiece of the dragons."

"And dragons breathe fire from their mouths!" he retorted. After a moment he sighed. "Ada, although the Oracle is a lantyn like you and me, she has a dragon living inside her. Think what that means. Dragons aren't pets who grant wishes, they are dangerous; creatures from another world with powers we don't understand. They are beyond us in every sense of the word. If they decided to destroy us, we wouldn't stand a chance, which is why it is a mercy that they've declared themselves our protectors...even if they don't appear to take the least interest in our struggles between each other. But that is probably better for us: they are fire and if you get too near to a fire you burn. That is why I was so worried about you." He broke off and looked away from her, out of the opposite window.

Ada bit her lip. He had been worried for her? She had no idea how to respond to that. Experience had taught her that anything she said would stoke, not calm, his rage; it was best to wait for the storm to end. Yet now he was silent. She waited, half-hope, half-dread.

They were almost home when he exploded again. "I'm angry for another reason. Can you tell me what it is?"

The question caught her off guard. She picked her words as carefully as she could. "Because I went off without asking you. And I'm too interested in things which threaten your position at court?"

His lip twitched.

"Elina told you that." He sighed. "No, dearest, the court gossips haven't stopped talking about how you tried to stay and listen to that Smoke Charmer. His words were deeply offensive to all drageldas, to all lantyns faithful to the dragons. In fact, this very morning, Callum proved that the old man was a Burning Heart."

Ada shivered slightly. Rishard had been right. Yet the Smoke Charmer hadn't seemed like a lunatic. Could there really be that much harm in a story?

Dura hadn't stopped speaking. "The Smoke Charmer was telling the Burning Hearts' version of the World's Greying. In case you hadn't realised it, accusing the dragons of enslaving all lantynkind goes against everything we live by. It is almost as good as treason. Don't nod and look sorry now – why did you listen to him for so long in the first place?"

"I was startled," Ada flashed. "It was so different from what I had heard before. I just wanted to know how his story ended."

"Ada," he ground out her name in despairing frustration. "When are you going to wake up? Survival at court demands sensitivity to your surroundings and responding appropriately, especially since the consequences aren't just limited to you. Do you think Rishard will want a wife who embarrasses him like this?"

"Rishard's already scolded me."

Dura grunted. "Then the boy has more sense than I gave him credit for."

Ada wished she were brave enough to return with a quick-witted scathing reply. *Why does everyone feel they have the right to tell me off for a bit of curiosity?*

"At least," Dura continued, "going to consult an Oracle clearly announced your allegiance to the dragons. Politically, it was a masterstroke. It will quell the rumours that you're sympathetic to Burning Hearts – yes, there are such rumours going around. But don't do it again – you nearly scared me to death."

After that, there was silence and the carriage trundled on. Ada thought that her father had finished, until they rounded the last corner and he asked, "What did the Oracle say?"

Briefly Ada explained the Oracle's prophecy and warning. She concluded: "...so I think I should get rid of my maid."

The carriage pulled to a halt.

Dura's eyes darkened. "Don't try to manipulate me, Ada. The maid stays."

"But the Oracle –"

"Oracle indeed. You've been pestering Kessler to get rid of that maid ever since your precious Meruda turned thief."

"She did not – you're lying!" The moment she said it Ada knew she had gone too far.

Her father's eyes burned, then hardened into stiff composure. "The maid stays," he repeated in icy coolness. "And I think that it is best that you stay within the house for the present. After your grand imaginings with the Oracle, it would be better for you to avoid court for a while, especially while the ambassadors from Nordlann are here. No daughter of mine is going to be an instrument of a Northman, no matter what any Oracle says."

11

Reports

"That's an apology for my shameful neglect of you."

Ada opened the box of sweetmeats Rishard had given her, fingers tingling. She couldn't remember the last time someone had spontaneously given her a present. Of course she would have preferred him to apologise about scolding her for listening to the Smoke Charmer. On the other hand, she missed having a friendly face to talk to: best not be sullen.

She smiled her thanks and popped one of the delicacies into her mouth, savouring the sticky sweetness. "I like your apologies. Here." She offered him one.

He sat down next to her on the arbour bench and accepted a bonbon with a grin. "Aww, how did you know? They're my favourites!"

Ada nearly choked. "So that's why you chose them!"

"Naturally. But that is not all I bring: I come with information." He turned and waved his attendant over. Ada had scarcely noticed the man; he had been a noiseless shadow.

“This is Sniffer,” Rishard said. “You remember, I promised to set him on the trail of your desperado kidnappers.”

Ada shifted. Although discomforted by Rishard’s melodrama, she examined Sniffer with interest. He did not meet her gaze, but let his eyes rove over their surroundings, examining the garden shrubs with deep suspicion. Despite the half-scowl, he looked familiar, having one of those faces that resemble a dozen acquaintances at once.

He spoke in a quiet drone. “Your description matches two rogues known as Daggers and The Giant. They often try this kind of thing: alleyway robberies, or snatching their victims down into the river tunnels if they have more finery to strip. They weren’t on their normal patch when they tried to take you, but the Watch has upped its guard where they used to work, so they were likely trying out a new territory and upset the local thief, the Silk Shadow, who must have decided it was more important to chase them off his turf rather than rob you.”

“So, I was both snatched and rescued by common thieves?”

Sniffer nodded.

“And where are these gentlemen with the ludicrous names now? Have you reported your findings to the Watch?”

Sniffer’s wandering eyes managed to find their way to her face. “I beg your pardon ma’am, but I thought you wanted me to be discreet. The Watch already know about these men and want to arrest them. If I go telling your story to the four winds...”

“Yes, you’re quite right,” Ada interrupted. “Thank you for your service.”

Sniffer jerked a bow and slunk away.

"How reliable is he?" Ada asked, nodding after Sniffer's retreating figure.

"I've never known him wrong yet. So set your mind at rest but stay away from shadowed alleys and lonely spots. I'd hate for you to disappear. I'm rather fond of you, you know."

Ada returned his smile, hiding her deflation. She hadn't wanted to be the victim of a sinister plot, but being one suggested more importance than falling prey to common robbers. Yet, what with Sniffer's report and the Oracle's promise of the dragons' protection, it was time for her to stop worrying about the kidnapping and move on.

Thinking of the Oracle reminded her of the prophecy. Rishard had talked about the tensions with Nordlann; perhaps he could help her find a way to resettle the peace.

She turned to Rishard but her questions evaporated as she met his gaze.

"What are you looking at?" she asked.

"You."

Ada felt the blood rush to her cheeks. She hid her embarrassment with a laugh. "But why?"

"I still can't believe your father actually gave permission for our betrothal. You are beautiful."

He meant it, she couldn't doubt it. She looked down at her lap, confused. She liked Rishard and enjoyed his company, but they still didn't really know each other yet.

She tilted her head, meaning only to look away, but she sensed his admiring gaze on her arching neck. He was absorbed with her. The small taste of power was intoxicating.

Power? The thought startled her. Her heart raced. She didn't want power like this, or did she? Or was she the one being succumbed by a few soft words? She needed time to think!

At the same moment she remembered Iris, who had been silently standing to the side this whole time. Ada's mind cleared at once. Whatever else, she wasn't going to make a fool of herself in front of that girl.

Ada looked straight into Rishard's face. "I've been wanting to ask you something."

A smile played with his lips. "Ask away."

"You said that Nordlann had conquered Errivel after planting discord in their court. You think they will try that here?"

Disappointment shadowed his face but he quickly rallied. "It's possible. They would need a significant advantage over us to attack. The Border Mountains in the north would funnel any invading force through the Great Pass; or if they tried attacking from Errivel to the east, they would have to cross the Derimere, either at the lake, which is wide; the river which is well fortified; or the swamps or Veiled Forest, any of which would be a dampener to their invasion plans."

"But you believe Nordlann means to attack?"

"Going by their conquests over the last ten years and the fact that we and our barbaric western neighbour Sendiva are the last independent states on this side of the Achille Sea, then yes, I think it's likely. There are already reports of their patrols overstepping the northern boundaries. All quite innocent of course, they're only trying to recapture fugitives, Burning Hearts and the like, but the repeated incursions are moving from accidental to an active challenge. His Majesty will have his hands full when those Nordish bigwigs arrive. The palace is already in mayhem preparing for their reception."

My servant from the north. The Oracle's words rang in her ears. Ada shivered. The prophecy was coming true! She would have to find a way to meet the Nordlannders, no matter what her father said. Peace depended on it. It was a shame not to tell Rishard about the Oracle so that they could work together, but she still stung from her father's reaction and didn't want to battle Rishard's scepticism.

"We could go to the ambassador's reception together?" Rishard looked at her hopefully.

"Yes!" She had sounded too keen; Rishard looked thrilled. Ada tried to tone down his delight by adding, "If father allows me to."

"Of course he will; I'll make sure he does. Now what about those bonbons? You've been holding that box all this time and you've only offered me one!"

Lord Dura tapped the wooden arm rest. "Did she believe you?"

Sniffer grinned. "Why shouldn't she? And anyway, most of what I told her was true."

"Apart from the fact that those two thugs were hired to kidnap her and you were her gallant rescuer."

"Yep." Sniffer helped himself to some wine and settled himself into one of the chairs, his legs sprawling easily in front of him. He raised his goblet. "To the Silk Shadow."

Dura raised an eyebrow. "The Silk Shadow?"

"The name I gave my alter ego. I like to enjoy some credit."

"Even under a false name?"

"I live under so many false names that credit to any of them counts the same. Although for a moment I thought she recognised me. She almost did at the Assembly of Artisans."

Dura gave him a keen glance. "You're sure she didn't?"

Sniffer threw him a hurt look. "What do you take me for? How many times have I met her over the years? And she still doesn't know who I am. If she could pin me down to one character it'd be the merchant, Jacques of Elipmnus, but she clearly didn't recognise Jacques. I almost wished I had appeared as him. She always had a smile for crazy Uncle Jacques."

Dura stared. "She calls you Uncle Jacques?"

"When in character as the merchant. He always had some toy, trick or joke for her. Does that bother you?"

Not deigning to answer, Lord Dura once more stared into space, his fingers beating a tattoo on the wood. His mouth slid into a wry twist. "By the way, how did your colleagues respond to your interfering with the kidnap?"

Sniffer spluttered. "Colleagues! We're more likely to cut each other's throats than talk to one another. But if someone is numbskull enough to employ us both and give us conflicting instructions...well I say, may the best man win. And of course, I did."

Dura nodded, his face impassive. "For which I thank you."

Silence.

"I notice your southern steward is still here," Sniffer commented.

"Yes."

"I've told you it's not safe for him to remain here. He's too innocent by half and he'll be used against you."

"That's why I want him close. If I sent him back south now, he'd be vulnerable on the road. Keep an eye on him. If trouble does come, try to get him out."

"I've only got two eyes you know. I can't watch everybody."

Dura got up and went to the window, staring down into the garden. The arbour was just visible. Ada and Rishard were laughing.

"They look happy," Sniffer observed. He had appeared by Dura's elbow.

"Are they happy? Have I chosen well for her?"

"Bit late to be consumed by doubts now." Sniffer slurped another mouthful. "But yes. They have as much chance of happiness as any other arranged marriage, and better long-term chances than many wild romances. He cares for her. He's not a totally obsessed, lovesick puppy and he's not stupid about how materially advantageous this match will be for him, but he does care for her. All the same, it's not the most prudent choice you could have made: his lands aren't that big, even if they do border yours."

"Some things are more important."

"Well, if you want Ada to be with someone who can love her, you've selected from her potential suitors with more kindness than most of your peers. But the boy is woefully inexperienced at wooing."

"That's one reason I like him."

Sniffer rolled his eyes. "Yes, but you're a stick in the mud. I've tried to give him a few pointers but I'm not sure how much the pig-head has taken on. He thinks he needs to prove himself by knowing everything. That breezy worldliness might impress some weaklings, but not your daughter. She wants to be accepted as an equal not patronised. She has a good mind and craves affection, you know. Or you *would* know if you hadn't shut her away down in Ilnora all these years."

Dura's eyes flashed. "She's yet to prove her mind to me. Since she's got here, she's displayed a reckless tendency: wandering into lonely alleys, getting abducted and trying to keep the whole thing a secret from me instead of asking for protection and investigation; she lingered to listen to heresy in front of a watching court; sneaked off to visit the Oracle. She's lucky she didn't become dragon-possessed! She's blundered from one danger to another without learning a thing. She acts without thinking of the consequences."

"Then perhaps someone ought to have taught her better...or *start* teaching her." Sniffer finished his goblet. "Anyway, things to do, people to watch." He sauntered out.

Dura returned to his silent vigil.

12

The Monster in the Mirror

Footsteps.

Ada meandered through the empty hallway, ears pricked. The awkward clump of boots stopped and started behind her. She was right: one of the gardeners was following her.

Ever since her excursion to the dragnoss, her father had given orders that she was to be restricted to the grounds and kept under constant watch. Rishard's intermittent visits were her only connection to the outside world.

Her precious father. He was the only one to whom she had told the Oracle's prophecy and what had he done? Assumed that she was lying and trying to manipulate him. It showed what he thought of her. He didn't even trust her to attend the private river party tomorrow hosted by his old friends Lord and Lady Kishere. But things would be different one day.

In the hope of preparing herself to work with the Nordish ambassadors, she ransacked maps and books for any scrap of information about Nordlann. The results were pitiful. She tried questioning Kessler, since she had a vague idea that his family came from Nordlann, but he could tell her very little. Instead he turned the conversation into a cross-examination as to how her new maid was settling in. And to think that her father said that *she* was pestering Kessler about Iris!

With no more resources to plunder, she had wandered over the gardens and house, wearing the lawn and floorboards thin as she worried over the prophecy. It was during these wanderings that the servants' constant shadowing had begun to irk her, and the passing days only increased her aggravation.

Ada stomped upstairs.

The footsteps followed.

She wheeled around, glaring. The gardener, halfway up the flight of steps, flushed bright red, looking so embarrassed that Ada nearly laughed.

Kessler rounded a corner. The pair of servants began an obvious pantomime, agreeing to switch shadowing responsibilities. Ada stalked away, her flash of humour evaporated. She didn't want to talk to Kessler.

More servants were coming down the corridor towards her. Without thinking, Ada barged through the first door on her right and closed it tight after her, leaning against the rough wood. She would not be followed anymore!

Moments passed.

No-one attempted the door.

Ada relaxed a little and considered her surroundings. She had not explored this way before. A series of steps spiralled up in front of her. Particles of dust danced in and out of the steep shaft of sunlight. Cool air whistled from above, carrying a pungent odour and a gentle cooing.

Curious, Ada climbed the stairs. She emerged into a turret room. Half the floor was raised like a stage and barred off, enclosing a few potted trees where perched a dozen pigeons: her father's messenger birds. That was why the servants hadn't followed her: no-one was allowed up here, including her. Ada glanced at the empty stairs. She was here now and a little blissful solitude wouldn't hurt: she would go down soon. She stepped towards one of the many slotted windows.

Ada gasped in delight at the vastness of the view. Below her was the courtyard and in the distance the spires of Vière Castle. She skipped to the opposite window: she could look down into their garden, the busy city streets and, raising her eyes, she could even spy the top of the Dragnoss Dome. She was on top of the world.

"What are you doing here?"

Ada spun around. Her father stood behind her, his eyes sharp. *Where had he come from?* She thought he was at Court.

"I...I was just exploring."

He nodded once, his face still blank. He stepped alongside her, gazing out on the city as she had done. Ada waited. The back of her neck felt hot, her palms moist.

"Court life can be..." His words flashed and trailed off like a shooting star.

Ada's heart rose: his frustration wasn't aimed at her. She kept silent, waiting for him to continue.

When he did, his voice had resumed its usual calm. "Your grandfather had this tower built specially to house his messenger birds. He learned the technique during his stay on the Elipmnus Isle. We Duras still use the method to communicate with our southern lands. This place...it's a thread to home."

Ada gave him a sidelong glance, hardly believing her ears. Her father got homesick?

He looked southwards. "These birds are precious. That's why I don't allow anyone up here."

Disappointed, Ada stepped back. "I'll go then."

"Why?" he asked. "I said *we* Duras. You're my daughter. This place is exclusively for our family use, a connection to our real home." He gave the room a wry glance. "This is the true private residence of our family. Glamorous, eh?"

Her father was joking with her? Ada gave a polite half-chuckle.

"Only don't try to handle the birds just yet; I'll show you in good time. Now I need to be off to court."

Ada took her courage in both hands. Her father had already denied Rishard's request about taking her to the reception for the Nordlann ambassadors, but if she proved herself at a lesser function, he might change his mind. And she might not catch him in such a good mood again. She moistened her lips. "Father, may I go to the Kishere's river party?"

His face did not change, did not even flicker. After a long pause he slowly shook his head. "Not just yet." He turned and descended the spiral steps. The door creaked open.

Kessler's surprised voice was answered by her father's reassurances. The door clanked shut.

Ada gazed at the spot where her father had appeared. How had he come there without making a noise? No-one had been in here when she arrived. She crossed the room and paused where he had stood. A slight breeze brushed at her dress. She knelt down, examining the spattered-white panels which lined the drop between the raised floor of the aviary and the floorboards of the lower half of the turret room.

She held up a hand and passed it in front of the panels. A gentle flow of air touched her hand. Ada cautiously pushed; first one panel and then the next. Something gave and a small square door silently opened inwards. The hidden hinges must be very well oiled.

Ada straightened and returned to the window which looked down on the courtyard. Her father was busy talking to the household chamberlain while a groom led up his black stallion Dester. He would be gone in a moment.

She turned back to the hatch-door, a black square patch luring her forward with the promise of secrets. Ada crouched down and peered in. It wasn't as dark as she thought it would be: pinstripes of light streamed down from between the thin cracks of the aviary floorboards, showing an interior which stretched out of sight. Ada went in.

Beyond the hatchway entrance there was plenty of room to stand, although the space was narrow. It was a passageway, snaking down around the outer wall of the tower. Things grew darker as she descended, although small gaps in the outer wall provided spots of light, while sounds of servants bustling and clattering came through the inner walls. Down and down the passage curved. Finally, it levelled out into a low-ceiling tunnel.

Stooping as she turned a corner, Ada was met by a bright green glow and a dank breeze. The floor ahead was a thick metal grating, with one of the river tunnels passing beneath, and after only a few paces the walkway ended in a solid wall. Vegetation trailed over the stones, illuminated through with sunlight. There must be a way up.

Ada tested her weight on the nearest part of the grating. It didn't so much as creak. She stepped forward with growing confidence.

The passage didn't end at the stone wall, but extended a short way to her right. Here there were metal pegs riveted into the stone which could serve as steps and handholds. She used them, climbing up to the wide-set bars and leafy canopy above.

Cautiously, Ada parted the foliage. She was at ground level of an empty street. She poked her head up a little for a better view and recognised the windowless wall opposite her. She had passed this spot before and had taken this patch of weeds and bars to be yet another common river drain.

What possibilities this opened up!

Her father rounded the corner on horseback.

Ada dropped down.

Dester's great hooves clopped nearer.

They shouldn't be coming towards her if heading to the palace. Why was he coming this way? Had he seen her?

Ada fled up the passage, up the steps and back through the hatchway. She checked it was shut securely, flew down the turret stairs, burst into the corridor – startling the waiting servants – and hurried back to her room.

Nothing happened.

Ada's racing heart slowed. Her spirits rose.

She had a way out of the house now. Even if Rishard couldn't arrange for her to go to the Nordlannder's reception, she could still make it. Beyond that, just knowing she could escape whenever she wanted to made everything feel better. Of course, it would be foolhardy to use it for anything less than an emergency, as every use would increase the likelihood of discovery. If her father found out...and yet, he had given her clear permission to be in the bird tower, and had made no effort to explain his sudden appearance. Had he meant her to find the passage?

Ada stroked the dragon necklace the Oracle had returned to her, lost in thought. That moment in the tower had been special. Her father had spoken to her like a real person, connected with her on the one thing they had in common: home.

Ada froze. *The one thing they had in common...*

That was what she needed to work with the Nordlann ambassadors, a common desire and interest. And the Oracle had already given her the answer to that: the dragons. In fact, serving the dragons was the whole purpose of their prophesied collaboration. How could she have been so dense? She could prepare by learning more about the dragons. The Oracle herself had said Ada ought to devote herself more fully to them, but how?

Her eyes gleamed. She had a copy of *The Light Lore.*

Ada hurried to the bookshelf. She hadn't thought about it since the Assembly of Artisans, but surely if a book-like object were delivered for her, it would have been placed here. Her fingers traced over the book spines: *The Dragon Fables, The Ballad of Nymkhet, Tales of the Elipmnus Knights.* She saw a glint of mirrorstone and pounced.

She drew it forward and opened the leather cover.

Pane after pane of sparkling crystal met her eye, each panel finely engraved with letters. It was exquisite craftsmanship. Yet the black velvet cloth needed to separate the pages was missing. Half-wondering if one of Iris's black serving caps would work as an alternative, Ada took *The Light Lore* to the bed, laid out full length on her tummy and reverently examined the mirrorstone.

...the Morning Star rises in your hearts.

The words jumped out at her, catching her eye from amid the crowds of sentences.

Morning Star. The phrase was familiar; one she had heard recently. She strained her memory but could not remember. It was only when she had given up and was beginning to re-examine the mirrorstone that it came back to her: it was a name the Smoke Charmer had used.

In his version of the World's Greying, he had said that the first lantyns had been filled with a light which he had called the Morning Star. That did not exactly contradict the way the dragnoss guardians told the story, but they never gave the original light any kind of special name. They focused on the dragons' promises to fill lantynkind with light once more, on "the-light-to-be" rather than the "light-that-was". Yet it was curious...Her father had said that the Smoke Charmer was a Burning Heart and as a Burning Heart – and thus a madman who rejected everything to do with the dragons – why had he used a name from *The Light Lore*, the basis of the Dragons' Creed? And since it was in *The Light Lore*, why had she never even heard a guardian mention the Morning Star? Perhaps the Smoke Charmer was mad or perhaps... what? Ada did not know.

Ada felt a little uneasy. Perhaps her father had been right and she was dabbling in things beyond her. Yet she had the dragons' favour (the Oracle had been quite clear about that) and wasn't it better to find out the truth for yourself?

She tried to re-read the bit about the Morning Star again, but she had lost her place. As she looked closer, she realised that the words could have come from any of the crystal pages. The sentences on each individual pane were fully formed and logical, yet *somehow*, when the panes were stacked together, all the words on all the layers of the crystal overlapped to form a perfectly coherent meaning.

Ada frowned. It was a very clever piece of work, one she didn't understand, but the words baffled her more than the design. She could see plenty of promises and prophecies about light shining out and consuming darkness, and it kept talking about something called the dark disease but as yet she couldn't find any descriptions about the dragons being the protectors of lantynkind, or any instructions about giving tribute.

Her spine prickled. Someone else was in the room. Ada looked up: no-one. She listened: silence.

She carried on reading with growing unease. Her instincts were screaming alarm, but she had no idea why. Something was wrong. Something was *wrong*...

She read on. A fresh line jumped out at her.

...the light has come into the world, and people loved the darkness rather than the light, because their deeds were evil.

She finally saw what was wrong. It had begun slowly, so imperceptibly that she had not noticed it at first: the words were shining. Not merely glowing, as any decent mirrorstone should, but the carved lettering was positively shining and growing brighter. The flick and curve of every letter was burning gold.

Ada watched entranced. There was something about that light, as if all beauty and goodness were contained within it and it was calling out to her. She felt as though she could never see enough of it and yet...Ada shifted uncomfortably, wishing the light would dim, just a little. It did not. The brightness grew to a searing white, burning the image of those words into her mind.

...the light has come into the world, and people loved the darkness rather than the light, because their deeds were evil.

Ada tried to look away but she was transfixed. The words, the light...*it* was holding her captive, compelling her, burning her. Panic surged into a wild hatred.

The words moved, actually *moved* across the page. Shining letters closed ranks until they were gathered together in the centre of the mirrorstone, then the white-gold pool of light condensed and lifted itself out of the mirrorstone, coalescing in the free air. The tendril of solidified light reached out and touched Ada's hand.

It hurt.

Ada started away but the light held her fast, clamping her hand in place as it pressed into her, cracking and blackening her skin. The arm of light grew brighter. The withering darkness crept up her arm.

It was draining her, pulling the life out of her. Ada tried to break free, but her arm was paralysed – even her voice was choked into silence. She could only watch horrified and helpless as that arresting grasp of light infected her with this...this dark disease.

A shadow beckoned her eye. Against her will, Ada's gaze was forced back to the mirrorstone book. The panels of crystal had changed: no longer light; instead, a dark monster watched her, eyes fixed on her hungrily, its glass skin blackened and twisted and beneath, instead of a deep skin, a darkness writhed and billowed like thunderclouds.

All the while the mirrorstone light shone yet brighter.

It wasn't just her hand or arm that hurt now, her whole being seemed to be on fire. She could feel the words searing into her very depths but now they were personalised.

You love darkness...your deeds are evil...

Ada shrank back. The monster mirrored her action.

O Mother Levia no! *It can't be.*

Yet it was: that vile thing was her reflection. As she looked, she no longer merely saw the crusting darkness but could feel it seeping into her, a poisoned rottenness hollowing her out, turning her into that monster.

The light pressed close.

She was the monster.

Ada screamed. She wrenched herself free and hurled the mirrorstone away.

It hit the stone floor and cracked.

13

First Glimmer of Madness

For an agonised moment Ada waited, then she peered down at the mirrorstone. It had landed face down and the cover completely hid the crystal. The eerie light had vanished.

She rubbed the skin on her arms, searching for any disfigurement. Everything was all clear and smooth once more. She realised that she was gasping for air, trembling.

What was that?

She put her head in her hands.

"Stupid girl," she muttered.

The door flew open and a couple of servants, headed by Iris, came running into the room.

"Are you all right, my lady?"

"We thought we heard –"

"Yes, yes," Ada replied curtly, remembering her scream with acute embarrassment. "I fell into a doze whilst reading and I had a bad dream." *Yes, that is all it was.* "I am sorry to have disturbed you and taken you from your duties. Please go back to them. I am quite well."

They filed out, all except for Iris who stood beside her.

"What is it?" Ada asked. *Why can't that girl just leave me be?*

"My duty is to look after you, my lady. Can I do anything to calm your spirits?"

"Some water please," Ada said, saying the first thing she could think of, trying to make Iris leave.

Iris made her way over to a side table where the water-jug reposed and proceeded to fill a horn beaker. As she turned around again, she caught sight of the mirrorstone lying abandoned on the floor. Without a word she picked it up. Surprise flickered across her face as she examined it. She looked up at Ada searchingly.

Ada ignored the silent enquiry, took hold of the beaker and started sipping with a dignified air, avoiding Iris's eye. All the same, she sensed the maid move to the bookcase near the door and slot *The Light Lore* back into its place.

"I hope, you enjoyed your reading, my lady," Iris said.

Ada whipped around with an irritable snarl but it died on her lips. Iris was glowing.

The hair on the back of Ada's neck prickled.

Diminutive, Iris stood waiting, head bowed, golden rays wafting out from her. The light spread through the room, seeming to reach out.

Ada stared, numbed. Once more she felt that simultaneous longing and horror. It was the same light from the mirrorstone, only this time it was coming from *inside* Iris, centred in her chest as a mass of gently pulsing light like...like a heart on fire. Ada's stomach plummeted. She had not known before the full meaning of those two infamous words:

"Burning Heart," she choked, her voice scarcely above a whisper. "You are a Burning Heart."

Iris started, looking up to meet Ada's eye. Another wave of light blushed through her, rippling through her crystal skin. "You can tell?" she spoke slowly, sounding oddly pleased.

"You are a Burning Heart," Ada repeated, her voice loud with disbelief, disgust and terror.

Iris stepped forward, her hands raised in a placating gesture, but Ada sprang off the other side of the bed, desperate to get away. Iris blocked the way to the door and was even now moving around the bed towards her. Ada ran to the fireplace, grabbed the poker and swung round, holding it out like a sword. "Stay back!" she ordered. "Stay back, or I'll scream for them to take you away."

Iris halted, "My lady, I –"

"Stop it," snapped Ada, as a fresh wave of gold blossomed from Iris. "Put it out. I don't want it touching me."

"Don't want what touching you?"

"That *light*."

Iris's eyes grew wider. "So you *can see*."

"First it was in that mirrorstone and now you – I said stay back," she cried again as Iris tried to advance, her hands still raised to pacify.

"My lady, it's me. I'm not going to hurt you."

"You're a Burning Heart," retorted Ada once again. No wonder the Oracle had warned her against Iris. All the same, it was incredible that Iris – Iris! – belonged to a cult of dangerous fanatics, especially as she stood there in mute patience, the picture of peaceful submission. But that serene glow declared her guilt. It was unnatural yet undeniably real. Some sorcery was at work here.

"How are you doing that?" Ada demanded.

Iris smiled; the first true smile Ada had seen her give. A dimple appeared in her left cheek. "Yhari lives in me."

"ihh-Yharr-ee?" Ada asked, trying to imitate the slight roll Iris had made. "What's Yhari?"

"Yhari is the Morning Star. He lives –"

"Morning Star?" Ada interrupted. That phrase was haunting her. She frowned, thinking back to what the Smoke Charmer had said. "You Burning Hearts think Yhari is this Morning Star, the original light?"

"He is the fire, the Living Fire that is meant to inhabit our hearts. The light you can see from my heart isn't me, it's him. And *The Light Lore* was written by him, that's why you saw him there."

Ada gaped, floundering for a reply. Timid, mouse-like Iris had put her finger on the crux of the matter. How could the dragons' sacred mirrorstone be filled with this *Morning Star*, the same light that apparently filled Burning Hearts? What was she missing?

Having waited in vain for Ada to respond, Iris pushed her further: "You don't believe *The Light Lore*, my lady?"

"How dare you." Whatever her experience, Ada knew *The Light Lore* was true and belonged to the dragons.

"Then you know that *The Light Lore* teaches us that we need fire in our hearts. The dragons and the guardians have twisted its meaning, promising light but never giving it. Whereas Yhari is the fire we need, and he can and does live in the hearts of all that call on him, within all Burning Hearts."

Ada felt totally at a loss. "But *The Light Lore* is the basis for the Dragons' Creed."

"Did you find that when you read it?" Iris asked.

Ada could only stare at the girl. Where did this boldness come from? It was as if Iris had become a completely different person.

"The guardians twisted the meaning of *The Light Lore* to invent the Dragons' Creed," Iris repeated. "They stop people reading it for themselves by telling us that they are the only ones who can understand the Lore. But *The Light Lore* isn't about the dragons, it's about Yhari. It says how our hearts were made for Yhari, and when he returns to his rightful place you can't keep it hidden – he shines out. He's the only one who can give light, who can break the curse and free us from the dark disease and the dragons' tyranny."

The light pulsated through Iris, stronger than before, refining and beautifying her features as it radiated through her to fill the whole room with exquisite splendour. It touched Ada.

Ada flinched at the burning sensation. "Why does it hurt?" she asked. "If it is meant to live inside of us why does it hurt?"

"Because his light exposes the dark disease within us."

The dark disease. That had been mentioned in *The Light Lore*. Ada recalled the twisted monster watching her within the mirrorstone, posing as her reflection. Ada shook her head. It couldn't be true. It must be a trick. She opted for attack. "What do you mean? I am not diseased."

"My lady, ever since our ancestors rejected Yhari, our hearts have become dark and that darkness has become engraved into our very bodies, and every action or thought that goes against Yhari only darkens us further, making us more inclined to stay in darkness. This is the 'dark disease'. But when Yhari shines we see what true light is, and when he shines on us it exposes what we have become and the contrast is painful. It's like stepping into dazzling sunlight from a dark cellar. His words and light act as a mirror to show us ourselves. He gives us synaiads to impress the truth on us, instead of the sirens who foster our delusions. It is a terrifying kindness, to show us how much we need him."

Ada leant against a chair. Her mind was whirling with so many reactions that she was sure the room was spinning. The predominate reaction was an internal screaming indignation at Iris's so-called explanation. If she understood her rightly, the girl was calling her and everyone else in existence an evil-hearted monster. But for all her outrage, Ada could not shake off the vision the mirrorstone had shown her, nor indeed the fact that Iris was glowing, nor the fact that what Iris said appeared to agree with what she had read in *The Light Lore*, far more than what the dragnoss guardians taught. There was a bizarre, outlandish sense to her version of reality.

Ada frowned, thinking hard. The pressing question was what was to be done now. Here, at last, was a foolproof reason to dismiss Iris. Her father would certainly not approve of her having a Burning Heart as a maid, but she doubted that he would believe her if she just told him. He would explode again, convinced she was trying to manipulate him.

A rebellious curiosity seized her.

Ada looked at Iris again. The girl was breathing fast but her face was calm, even if her eyes were downcast.

For the first time, it occurred to Ada what would happen to Iris if she were dismissed. She had no idea what family or security Iris had, and publicly exposing the girl for being a Burning Heart would likely bring life-long disgrace and ostracism. The girl had never shown violent tendencies and whatever the strange things some Burning Hearts might do, Iris was obviously (and surprisingly) a moral, rather than a violent, radical.

The danger lay in that Yhari thing. She shuddered slightly at the memory of the mirrorstone light. The dragons had preserved her but she wouldn't run that risk again; she would never again try to read *The Light Lore*.

As for Iris, she might prove useful in teaching her about Burning Hearts. Then she might understand why Nordlann reputedly hated Burning Hearts even more than her own society did. And if she spoke to the Nordlann ambassadors they would see that she understood their concerns: they would respect her and listen to her. Yes, Iris may prove useful, but she would have to learn to hide that hideous light.

Ada let the poker drop (secretly quite glad, for it had been getting heavy).

"I don't think," she said, "that anyone should know that you are a Burning Heart. It would only cause trouble."

Hope glimmered in Iris's eye.

"And I would like to hear more of your...ideas," Ada went on. "But you must keep your light under control. You've clearly done it before; I expect you to do so again."

"I don't control him my lady, he has his own will."

"Then I suggest you persuade him that it's in both your interests that he keeps himself hidden: no-one must find out what you are, especially not my father. Or Kessler for that matter. What, pray, is so amusing?"

Iris bubbled with laughter. "Kessler won't report us," she said.

"He is my father's steward," retorted Ada. "He would consider it his duty to tell my father. Once and for all, why are you laughing?"

Iris didn't speak but smiled meaningfully.

Some of the old frustration began to simmer – *why couldn't Iris just say what she meant?* – when understanding broke in upon Ada like a flood.

"Kessler? A Burning Heart?"

Iris nodded.

The bottom of her world dropped out. Ada staggered backwards into a chair, head reeling. It fitted. In all the years she had known Kessler, she couldn't think of one occasion when he had offered dragon tribute, attended the teachings from Guardian Rosquebelle or even voluntarily mentioned dragons, not even to swear by them. How had she missed it?

She was sad he had never told her. Of course, it was sensible of him to have kept his peculiarity a secret, but it hurt that he hadn't trusted her with it. Did her father know?

It was hard to imagine him not knowing something like that, and yet she could not imagine him knowingly employing a Burning Heart, particularly in such a trusted position.

With the thought came a new confidence. If she had managed to cope with the close proximity of a Burning Heart all these years (albeit unwittingly), then it meant that she could find a way to cope with Iris. It must all be part of the dragons' plan.

14

Coming and Going

Ada rushed to the window at the sound of the carriage wheels. It was only her father leaving.

"Please my lady, I haven't finished your hair."

For once Ada meekly submitted and followed Iris back to the dressing table.

Today was the day when everything would change. She had received a royal invitation to the reception of the Nordlann ambassadors (how had Rishard managed it?) and her father could not refuse the king. Any moment now, Rishard would arrive and take her to the palace. She wouldn't need to use the tunnel: it was all coming together.

She could hardly keep still. Energy thrummed through her, down to her very fingertips. Was she ready? Would she know what to do and when to do it? She tried to silence the riot of questions. If the dragons had placed their confidence in her, how could she not be confident in herself? When the time came, she would know what to do.

Besides, she had prepared as best she could, reading and re-reading everything she could find on dragons –

apart from *The Light Lore* – and had quizzed Iris about her convictions. Although her conversations with Iris proved more confusing than helpful: her ideas were fascinating to listen to, but afterwards Ada couldn't remember half of it and understood even less.

What she did remember was Iris's radiance; when she spoke about Yhari, the light intensified, its beauty transmuting Iris's glass skin into loveliness. Her newfound confidence was disconcerting too. Ada would never have believed that the girl could be so confident about anything, yet she could happily spout dragon treason by the hour. What was more, her evident joy in talking about Yhari only strengthened her shining beauty.

All the same, Ada never forgot the memory of the light's searing touch and kept a wary distance. The light suited Iris and she could even be pleased for her maid (dragon-heretic though she was) but it was not for her.

"You're looking forward to the reception," Iris stated.

"I am." Ada afforded her a gracious smile. "It's going to be a grand event to welcome our Nordish guests, Prince Ellis and Lord Saupa." Did she imagine it or did Iris's hands tremble a little?

"And you are more eager to meet them than to enjoy the celebrations?" Iris asked.

"That's very perceptive of you. Yes. You find that surprising?"

Iris paused and, as usual, didn't answer the question directly. "They are intimidating men. At least Lord Saupa is."

Ada turned to stare up at Iris. "How do you know anything about him?"

"He is well known among Burning Hearts. Many have fled from him into Aven to escape his butchery. He is a fierce defender of the dragons and hates Yhari and everything to do with him."

"Oh." Ada turned away. "I think that's enough on the hair." Iris's quiet way of talking could be so compelling that Ada often forgot that the girl was spouting dragon treason. Moments like this jarred her back to reality. For however gentle Iris might be, they were meant to be enemies – according to the dragons. Saupa was undoubtedly a zealous dragelda and Iris's version of him was likely drawn from criminals he had pursued, criminals who had taken their revenge in rumours, transforming Saupa into a monster. As such, Ada felt she was duty-bound to defend him.

"Hostility to Yhari is to be expected from a loyal servant to the dragons. But since the Oracle says I am to work with Lord Saupa, or someone from the north, I dare say we'll get along fine, however intimidating others may find him."

The hairbrush clattered to the floor.

Ada spun around.

Iris's face was white, her expression blank. She looked as if she were about to faint. Ada leapt up and forced Iris to sit in her place. Iris obeyed.

"What's wrong?" demanded Ada.

Iris swallowed several times before she could speak. "The dragons want you to work with Saupa? *That's* what the Oracle told you?"

Ada laughed at the petty reason for Iris's shock, but stopped as she looked at the girl's face again: Iris really was shaken. She tried to speak gently. "Yes but that's a good thing: we're going to bring peace to the southern realms. Why? Don't you believe in prophecies?

"It depends on who's making the prophecy. False prophecy is a lie for manipulation."

Ada's anger stirred. Who was Iris to preach about being deceived: she was a Burning Heart! But before she could say anything, she heard the distant call for the gates to be opened. Rishard must be here. All other thoughts vanished.

Ada rushed back to the window which looked down on the courtyard. It was him. She flew downstairs and through the hall to assume her rightful, central position. Her excitement had returned in a flood: she couldn't help bouncing on the balls of her feet.

The carriage wheeled into the outer courtyard, sending small stones pinging to either side and servants scurrying out of its path. Some of the household staff spilled out of the doorway to join the line of respectful welcome.

Before the horses had been reined to a complete halt, Rishard had opened the carriage door, leapt down and bowed so deeply – his left hand tumbling through the air in mad flourishes, his right leg scraped back dangerously far – that he was nearly floored by his own flamboyancy and speed. Yet he managed to catch himself before total prostration and, righting himself with a grin, he extended a hand. "My lady, your carriage awaits."

Laughter echoed from within the carriage. The faces of Laurence Halbert and his mother, Lady Marguerite il Kishere appeared in the aperture, smiling.

Ada returned their greetings.

"I hope you don't mind us all going together," Lady Marguerite said. "But it is ridiculous to travel individually; the palace stables will be clogged up as it is. Besides, Rishard is obviously in danger of flattening himself if we don't keep an eye on him."

Ada joined in the general laughter and took Rishard's hand. She threw a farewell look backwards towards Kessler only to find herself smiling at that supercilious chamberlain. With her father already departed for the King's Council, it was Kessler's responsibility to see her off and he never shirked the smallest duty, so where was he?

The chamberlain gloated. His every feature showed pleasure at Kessler's failure.

Reality shifted.

He was no longer a lantyn but a monster. His form had twisted. His outer crystalline skin warped. Within him a dark cloud was swelling, pushing against his glass skin from the inside. It was just like her reflection within the mirrorstone.

Ada blinked.

The chamberlain was a normal lantyn again: glass skin a little greasy but otherwise normal.

Heart pounding, Ada looked away, blindly following the pull of Rishard's hand. What was happening to her? Was this Yhari's work? But if it was...No! She pushed the thought away, not daring to think through the implications. Today was too important for her to be distracted.

It was only as she was about to step up into the carriage that a slight disturbance near the gate caught her attention. There was Kessler, the new vision of Kessler that she could not get used to. Light transfused him. His slight stoop and grizzled locks were overridden with grandeur. He radiated nobility. Yet he also looked exactly the same. Perhaps she had always sensed the difference, but had not been able to physically see it before.

Kessler reached forward. He was speaking to a raggedy youth who was obviously begging.

It was a common sight. Beggars poured into Casida from all over Aven, vainly hoping that the capital would cure them of their poverty and rags.

Really Kessler, you're too soft for your own good.

Ada took a deep breath to summon him back from the brink of good intention when the lad shifted his position. The motion made him rotate to reveal his farther shoulder and the little girl who was clinging to it. There was something about her...maybe it was simply the combined effects of hollowed cheeks, overlarge eyes and the limp strands of muddied blond hair, or perhaps it was her shadowy resemblance to a long-buried memory. Either way it touched Ada. She was surprised at how much.

Rishard handed her into the carriage and, insisting that she should not risk creasing her pretty dress by shifting to make room for him, went around to the door on the other side.

A sudden impulse made Ada lean out of the window and call for Iris. She lowered her voice as the maid stepped forward.

"Have Kessler bring that little girl and her keeper in. He can use whatever he needs to make them comfortable. And tell him that the next time he chooses to usher in beggars, instead of saying goodbye, I shall have to speak to him most severely."

"Is there a problem?" Lady Marguerite asked.

"Not anymore," Ada replied, smiling as Rishard entered the carriage and settled himself down next to her. Her normal sight had returned.

15

Hunters on the Scent

Iris followed the rattling wheels to the gate, trying to avoid the choking clouds of dust they left in their wake. She spotted the exact moment when Kessler realised his negligence and winced at his belated bow. Then again, Lady Ada had obviously already forgiven him.

Iris did not feel jealous, only resigned. Her mistress loved the steward and only tolerated her. *If I served her faithfully for a hundred years, she would still throw a tantrum if her bath was a fraction too cold.*

When Iris relayed Ada's message, Kessler beamed and the young man with him almost collapsed with relief. Both Iris and Kessler rushed forward to support him and Kessler tried to take the little girl, but the child gave a soundless scream and tightened her hold on her protector.

"Better if I carry her," the stranger said, his voice hoarse yet with an unmistakable lilt.

Iris recognised the Nordish accent and examined the bedraggled pair with fresh interest. She had met several Burning Hearts who had fled from Nordlann's persecution, but if this pair were refugees, why had they come to a rich lord's house instead of seeking out the local gathering of Burning Hearts? Yet there were more pressing matters: the young man looked as if he could faint at any moment.

Together they led the strange duo inside. Sitting them down in an unoccupied corner of the kitchen, Kessler went to fetch some food. Iris was glad he went. The kitchen staff always huffed whenever Iris asked them for anything, even when it was for Lady Ada. But they respected the chief steward.

Iris concentrated on coaxing the girl to loosen her hold around her protector's neck. Slowly, with many gentle whisperings on her part and encouragement from the lad, the child released her grip and let Iris take her onto her lap.

After a little wait, Kessler returned with two steaming bowls and large hunks of bread and cheese, none the worse for his encounter with the cook, and the pair eagerly set to, although Iris took control of the little girl's spoon, afraid she would scald herself.

After blunting the edge of his hunger, the young man introduced himself as Kelvin and the girl as Orla, and he began to tell his story. At first, he spoke slowly in halting Avenese, interjecting the odd pause as he took another mouthful, but as he went on, he grew more assured and fluent. Kelvin described how he had been visiting his parents' grave in his birthplace, Marsen Strau, when he had met Orla's family. They had known his parents and welcomed him into their home. A few days later, an imperial patrol arrived and began to arrest people. Anyone who questioned the patrol or showed the least sign of resistance was killed. Panic ensued. Orla's father and brothers were killed in the madness. Kelvin, Orla and Orla's mother managed to escape. They saw the smoke rise as the imperial patrol razed Marsen Strau to the ground. Imperial patrols started to scour the woods and the three of them fled southwards towards the Avenese border, but while they were crossing the Border Mountains, Orla's mother had fallen and broken her leg, succumbed to a fever and died. Kelvin had buried her while Orla slept.

Iris had heard many such stories but she still keenly felt its horror, all the more for the expressionless voice in which Kelvin told it. She held Orla close, glad that the girl couldn't understand their language.

Kelvin went on: describing how the imperial patrols had pursued them even across the border into Aven; of how the shepherds had helped them and smuggled them onto wagons bound for Casida, right under Saupa's nose.

"But Saupa travelled down with the wagons. We managed to keep hidden and out of sight of his men but one of Sir Endric's men decided...how do you say?...to sell us out. But we overheard and we slipped away in time and made the rest of the journey by walking. It was not too far by then. We entered the city this morning and have been asking for Dura's house ever since."

"But why here? Why the house of Dura?" Kessler asked.

"Before Milah - Orla's mother - died, she asked me to search for her sister's husband, Edouard, who served the Lord Dura: he is Orla's uncle."

Iris was still scrabbling to form a mental picture of the family tree, but Kessler was nodding.

"Yes, Edouard was my father. He met and married my mother when accompanying the previous Lord Dura to Nordlann."

Orla nuzzled her head into Iris's shoulder. Iris stroked her hair, awed at the connections being revealed. Of course, there was no such thing as pure chance, only coincidences with purpose. Yet this was some coincidence. What was Yhari going to do here?

Kessler continued, "My mother used to speak of her home country and her little sister Milah, but it was so far away I never thought I would meet any of them. And now it seems that you have brought me my last surviving cousin. I am deeply in your debt. I will see to it that both you and Orla are provided for."

Kelvin hesitated a moment then pressed on. "I am very grateful, but I must speak to your master. He is the Lord Dura, yes?"

"Yes, but he's at court. Don't worry yourself; I can make whatever arrangements are necessary."

"I need to speak to him, most urgently."

"What about?"

But there Kelvin fell silent and couldn't be made to say anything more.

Iris had long waited, itching in puzzlement, for this suitable pause. "Didn't Orla have any relatives in Nordlann you could take her to?" she asked. "It's incredible what you've done but surely, the distance, the difficulty of coming here...?"

"Orla is a goldenhead," said Kelvin, nodding towards the girl's blond tresses. "The guardians patrol the villages for goldenheads. They take them to work" – he spat extra meaning into the word – "in the dragnoss. They punish you if you try to hide a goldenhead."

"Was that why the village was attacked?" Iris asked.

A painful grimace rippled over Kelvin's face, but he shook his head. "Many of us were...how do you say? *Loisg cridhe.*" He patted his hand on his chest in the rhythm of a heartbeat. "Yhari?"

"Oh." Iris understood. *He's a Burning Heart.*

Kessler understood too: he leant forward and lowered his voice as other servants started to flood into the kitchen. "Best not tell anyone else that; we don't know who might be listening. We will talk more later. Iris, take the child upstairs and see to her. A warm bath and some fresh clothes would do her good."

That was easier said than done: Orla was so afraid of losing sight of Kelvin, that at the first sign of Iris trying to take her away, she lurched forward and clung to him more tightly than ever. He murmured a stream of soothing reassurances in Nordish into her hair, hugging her close. Iris added her voice to his, albeit in Avenese, but she knew her tone was the important thing. Eventually Orla quietened and let Iris carry her upstairs to one of the lesser guest rooms.

Once there, Iris set about preparing a bath in the side room, assisted by a couple of maids Kessler sent to help ferry water. Orla had watched the process with great interest (almost as much interest as the other maids showed in her) but when the time came for her to undress and get into the tub, she erupted into an unintelligible stream of frantic words: she would *not* take off her clothes with Iris watching. After much patient miming and coaxing, Iris held a chemise over Orla like a tent, while the old clothes were awkwardly wrestled off by their young owner and kicked away over the floor. After many stumbles against Iris, Orla reached up her arms and let the chemise be dropped over her like an overlarge white dress. The great moment had arrived. Solemnly, Orla let Iris lift her up, over the rim and lower her into the tub. She stood up to her knees in water, staring at how the material puffed up and floated on the surface. Then she giggled, jumped and spun around, watching the water churn and dress spin as it floated.

Iris smiled, unusually tired, but pleased at her success.

However, trying to wash Orla proved to be harder than teaching a cat to swim. But such things do not last forever and once the painful scene of scrubbing had finished, the reproachful yowls and struggles morphed back into such giggles and excited splashes that Iris's dress was soaked.

I'll need to change too, Iris thought. It then dawned on her for the first time that she had no fresh clothes for Orla. Iris kicked herself. Normally she would have been laying out clothes whilst the mistress bathed herself, but that had not been possible with Orla.

Iris hoisted Orla out of the bath, swaddled her with towels and gestured for her to wait until she returned before hurrying to the linen rooms. There were no children-sized clothes anywhere, of course there wouldn't be. The only children in this mansion included a few stable-boys and kitchen skivvies, who wouldn't have any clothes to spare. She carried on searching, peeling back layers of neatly folded material to search further down.

Something nudged at her mind, but Iris ignored it, focusing on her problem instead. The nudging grew stronger, becoming less of a nudge and more of a pull, demanding attention until Iris couldn't ignore it. When she finally turned her thoughts towards it, recognition flooded through her. *Oh it's You! I'm sorry I wasn't listening.*

The pull turned into an urgent tug. *Danger. Need to go.*

What possible danger could there be? Iris reasoned, crouching down. *I'll just check this bottom shelf; it's the last one.*

A sudden idea entered her head: might some of the Lady Ada's childhood dresses be sentimentally tucked away somewhere? Well, if they were, they wouldn't be here. Iris rose hurriedly and headed back to Lady Ada's chambers.

As she passed along the corridor, a muted explosion of angry voices drew her to the window. Through the slight distortion of the glass, Iris saw a crowd of soldiers in strange armour trying to force their way through the gates. Dura's doormen were holding them back with angry protests and defiant yells. Other workers, drawn by the commotion, also ran to the gate to help defend their master's property. Then, quite suddenly, from the ranks of the attackers, a small contingent of the royal guard stepped forward. At their head stood a herald in a tabard of royal livery. Both sides untangled themselves and stood back to hear the herald read.

If only I could hear, Iris wished, straining her ears. *This pesky glass, you can't hear a thing.*

She glanced around to see if any of the nearby windows had an opening latch but something else caught her eye. Iris froze.

Sitting on the opposite roof, wings taut and poised, its neck extended down towards the scene below, was a dragon. Its breath came out of its mouth in a blue vapour, but instead of fading into the air, the mist streamed steadily down to hang in a thick cloud over the men below.

Iris knew that nobody else could see the monster and its poisonous breath. Those poor fools below were blind to this side of reality and had no idea how much of their lives were spent on a knife edge, no idea where the true peril lay.

She groaned to herself as she realised what Yhari had been warning her about in the linen cupboards. *I'm sorry. I should have listened*, she mentally called to him. *Please don't let the dragon see me.*

Slowly, she started edging her way down the passage, glancing down out of the windows as she went. The herald had finished speaking and Dura's men, with reluctance, stepped aside to let the intruders pass. The strangely-armoured men broke up into smaller units and deployed themselves through different doorways, leaving a couple to guard the exits. This was a manhunt.

Iris's mind flew back to Kelvin's story. She didn't know how, or even if, it was connected, but all her instincts told her that they were after two stray Burning Hearts.

Orla.

Iris squinted back to the roof. The dragon was staring straight at her, its coal-eyes glowering in recognition of an enemy. It rocked back then launched forward, swooping across the courtyard towards her.

Iris didn't waste any more time. She sprinted down the hall. Behind her the dragon passed through the solid walls without a sound and charged after her. She could feel its hot, putrid breath as it snapped at her heels.

"Yhari, help!"

Something bright flashed behind her and she heard a frustrated roar, but she kept running, not daring to look back until she reached Lady Ada's room. Only in the doorway, did she dare peek back down the corridor. It was empty, but it wouldn't be for long: she could hear the search party approaching.

Breathing silent thanks and pleas for continued protection she skidded over to a great wooden chest where Ada stored keepsakes. Iris heaved it open and rifled through the contents, overturning the neat piles and spilling them onto the floor. Old toys, favourite books, a gilded fan...

There must be something in here.

A scented candle, old pieces of needlework, a dried garland of flowers and...Yes. She let the fabric fall loose to check that she was right. Finally, she had found what she was looking for: a small red velvet dress with a gold threaded lattice over the waist and loose lace cuffs. The studded pearls made the dress a little too grand for every day wear, even for a little lady, but the rich did what they liked in such matters. Besides it was a big day at court where all the nobility would be decked out like peacocks and may allow their children at home to be dressed likewise.

She flew back to the door and down the corridor, almost tripping over her skirts. An undercurrent of worry eroded her elation of a moment ago. What was her plan? Hustle Orla out of the house in front of all the soldiers and servants, as if she were going to court? It would all fall flat on its face. Too much relied on the soldiers' perceptions and the servants holding their tongues.

The intruders' clamour chased her, their noise swelling in volume every second. They were getting nearer. Trying to drown out the sound and her own worries, she ploughed recklessly forward, running into a manservant as she turned a corner and knocking his arms open, sending wood logs clattering to the ground. He gave an indignant shout and Iris called a hasty apology over her shoulder, desperately hoping that the noise wouldn't attract the search-party below.

She ran around another corner, up a short flight of stairs, into the guest bedroom and into the side room.

Orla had gotten cold. To remedy this, she was struggling back into her old rags. With a groan of compassionate frustration, Iris whisked Orla's old clothes off and thrust them into the fire, using the poker to hide the garments under the smouldering logs. The soldiers mustn't find that. The old clothes had left some fresh grime on their owner.

Iris worked quickly, wiping the dirt marks off, rubbing the child dry and yanking the dress on.

They came before she was ready. She heard the door in the adjacent room fly open and the commands and bustle that followed.

Iris rushed to the door that stood between them and these hunters. Oh, why hadn't she locked it?

They beat her to it and the door was flung wide open.

Orla gave a little shriek and pulled up the dress that was half-hanging off her. Then, to Iris's astonishment, the little girl set her feet squarely apart and glared up at the soldier who towered above them in the doorway.

Iris imitated her stance. "How dare you come in here? Who gave you leave to tramp in here and disturb me and my charge? No-one, that's who. So go on, get out. Out!"

The man wilted before this tirade whilst his companions peering from behind smirked as they spotted the empty bath tub. This only gave fresh fuel for Iris, who began to berate them for their lack of respect and propriety, forcibly shooing them out of the room.

"And don't think that my mistress won't report this to the master. Then you won't find it so funny. You'll rue the day you came bursting in upon the little lady when she's bathing." With that she slammed the door in their faces.

There was a dead silence in the next room for a moment, followed by muffled sniggers, angry whispers and, finally, retreating footsteps.

When she was sure they were gone, Iris collapsed into a chair, completely drained, stunned at her own outburst.

Orla, who had figured some way to fix the dress on (if not quite the way its designer had originally intended) came over and rested a hand on Iris's lap. A smile dawned over her face as she began to laugh and chatter, a contented glow of pure light radiating from within. Iris picked her up, enjoying the childish sound, and began to arrange the dress properly.

She smiled for Orla, but there were too many sinister points about the episode for her to join in with the laughter. She did not know much about heraldry, but she knew enough to recognise the symbols of the key figures at court and she hadn't recognised the insignia that those men wore. Yet they had had royal support, which only deepened the mystery as to who they were working for. And what or who were they after. They hadn't looked twice at Orla. Maybe they had not even been looking for her but were after something else entirely. She remembered that moment, back in the kitchen, when Kelvin had asked to speak to Lord Dura and refused to tell Kessler why. Iris felt her insides go cold with understanding: they were after Kelvin. He must have had a message or something for Lord Dura, and now, unless Kessler had managed to get him out...She shuddered inwardly, feeling helpless.

Orla began to play with Iris's hair.

Overwhelmed with emotion, Iris hugged her tight. However this troublesome mess unfolded, she would do everything in her power to keep Orla safe.

16

Scandal

"Do you think," began one of the girls, fidgeting in her seat, "that Prince Ellis wants a bride? They could seal the peace agreements with a marriage."

"Don't get any grand ideas, my dear," chuckled the Lady Elina el Rienna. "He's a Brach'un Prince, not a Kil'jun Prince. In Nordlann, only the Kil'jun Princes are of royal blood. Brach'un Princes are simply Lords forming the Imperial Council. Much like the difference between 'el' or 'il' in our kingdom."

The information was received with disappointment and yet had very little impact, as they began to plan various campaigns of flirtation, convinced that each one would inevitably result in a wedding. Elina, evidently highly amused, pointed out that there was only *one* Prince for them all to marry. The chatter continued unabated.

Ada shifted, bored. This was not how she had envisioned court life. Is that what her father had meant to say to her in the pigeon tower? But at least he was doing things in the King's Council, while she was stranded outside among the airheads, with no prospect of personally meeting the ambassadors.

If only there was someone sensible to talk to: Rishard and Laurence had been summoned over to speak to Lord Kishere; she had been separated from Lady Marguerite in the crowds; and when Elina el Rienna had found her, she had insisted on introducing Ada to girls her own age. Growing up in the southern seclusion of Ilnora, Ada had rarely mixed with peers of her own rank and age. Judging by the current sample she hadn't missed much.

How long would she have to wait? Her tummy churned in anticipation. The Nordish ambassadors had already come and were in conference with King Rencival and his council while she was stuck out here with the rest of the nobility waiting for the festivities to begin. That would be her chance to meet them, but what was she meant to say? How was their alliance meant to begin? If only the prophecy had been more precise. She felt like she was waiting for a test, but didn't know what form it would take. She even had a horrible feeling that the test might have already started without her knowing it.

The short glimpse she had got of the ambassadors had not allayed her nerves. She began to have more sympathy with Iris's reaction.

All the foreigners she had met before were travelling merchants, such as Liccoshi of Kneab or Jacques of Elipmnus. They coaxed and flattered, trying hard to please and elicit favour, whereas these Nordish ambassadors were masters of the subtle insult. Their manners were gracious but suggested condescending superiority. Their clothes were all efficient elegance, well cut but plain, in stark contrast to the lavish pomp of the Avenese nobility. Her own regalia now felt heavy and uncomfortable. Moreover, they were a stern-looking lot with clean-shaven, unsmiling faces, their wide brows, distinctive long noses and the uniform haircut that was slightly too long for good Avenese taste. They did not look like the easiest people to talk to.

"Now what are you thinking of Ada il Dura?" Elina stood in front of her, blocking her off from the rest of the group.

Ada started back and nearly overbalanced into a lily pond.

Tripping was a constant peril of the indoor water gardens, with its irregular terraces ascending from the central walkway and with the lily ponds that had been designed to lie level with the paving. It was one of the lavish and impractical extensions that mad King Josét (Rencival's great-grandfather) had added to the old castle. He had meant it to be a tranquil haven for thinking, yet it was anything but tranquil when filled with courtiers fighting for foot room.

Ada saved herself from an unexpected swim and answered quickly to cover her embarrassment. "I was thinking about the ambassadors. I've not seen men from the north before."

Elina laughed. "Just about the ambassadors, eh? And what do you think of these men from the north? Which one did you think the most handsome? Come now, don't blush – you're not married yet. Besides, beauty is there to be admired in whatever form it presents, why else would I get Rencival to invite you here today?"

“Oh. Thank you.” Ada knew her thanks sounded deflated, but she had thought it was Rishard who had managed to get her invited to court. Who had she been fooling? Rishard was hardly high enough in the pecking order to whisper in the king’s ear.

“Never mind that,” Elina said. “I heard about your father cooping you up and I thought it was a right shame. But come now, answer me: which of those Nordlannders do you like the look of?”

Ada floundered, struggling to free herself from her preoccupation with the Oracle’s prophecy. “Well, um... Prince Ellis is handsome.”

“Ye-es,” said Elina dismissively. “He has the fairy-tale good looks I suppose, but I think his companion is much more interesting.”

“The Lord Saupa?”

“Yes, him.”

“He’s a bit short and...old.”

“Tut-tut,” Elina said sternly. “You should know better than that. I grant you that he’s not very tall but old? Well, maybe for you. But there’s something intriguing about him: he radiates power – you can see it in the way he walks – yet he acts so meekly, letting Prince Ellis have all the attention. I am sure that he knows the exact limit of his authority down to the slightest intonation and syllable of speech.”

Ada thought that was a lot to conclude from such a brief observation. She opened her mouth to say so when a scream ripped through the air.

The hall was abuzz, everyone looking around. The sound of a steady tramp drew everyone's eyes down towards the central walkway that led to the council chambers.

Like everybody else, Ada was straining her neck, vying for a spot where she could see what was going on. Through the shifting sea of people, she caught fleeting glimpses of Prince Ellis's guardsmen. Further gaps in the crowds gave her fragments of the scene below, but not enough to make sense of it until someone in front of her stepped down onto a lower terrace. She saw at once what was happening.

How dare they?

A deep powerful anger surged through her, making her shake with indignation. She was an earthquake of fury. *How dare they?* Ada surged forward, forcing her way through the massing throng, ignoring Elina's and everyone else's protests, until she burst onto the central pathway just in front of the guardsmen.

"Stop!" Her voice rang with furious authority, startling them into obedience.

The soldiers had been marching in a quadrangle formation as they all but dragged two bleeding, broken bodies. Ada gazed down at Kessler's semi-conscious form, then levelled her gaze directly into the commander's eyes and demanded, her voice trembling with anger. "What is the meaning of this?"

The captain didn't answer but bowed low, looking beyond her.

Ada turned around. The entirety of the King's Council – along with the ambassadors from Nordlann – were emerging from the inner chambers to see what the commotion was about. Her heart nearly fluttered to a stop as King Rencival strode to the head of the group and met her gaze. He halted. They all halted.

Ada gracefully curtsied down to the floor.

"Your Majesty."

Silence hovered.

"Prince Ellis," said Rencival. "Would you care to explain why your escort have assaulted my subjects and then dragged them into my court?"

"Your Majesty will remember," said Prince Ellis, "that when we first arrived, we requested permission to hunt down certain outlaws who had fled our borders and we believed had taken refuge in this city. And you most graciously agreed."

"Your men have been most prompt," the king replied. A slight edge in his voice tainted the compliment. "But in Aven we don't disrupt council sessions with petty policing."

"The fault lies with me, Your Majesty," Lord Saupa said.

It was the first time Ada had heard him speak. His accent was the clearest of all the Nordlannders and although his voice was soft, it rang with an assertion that Prince Ellis lacked. As he spoke his eyes steadily bored into Ada. They were so dark they were almost black.

Ada repressed a shiver. Elina was right: this man held power and knew how to use it.

Her dreams of an instant golden relationship withered.

Saupa continued, breaking eye contact with Ada as he turned back to face King Rencival. "I did not make it sufficiently clear to the captain what should be done with these criminals once caught. I humbly beg your pardon for such a careless oversight. Please continue the council. I will ensure that they are secured elsewhere."

With barely concealed impatience Rencival nodded his head in permission and his company turned back towards the council chambers. The watching courtiers turned to each other in murmured conversations and rustling movement ran through them like a gentle breeze.

Ada looked around despairingly. They can't just take Kessler like that! She summoned all her courage. "My Lord King."

Silence dropped like a wet blanket, smothering the newborn wave of noise. Everyone stared at her.

Ada's mind went blank. She could only see Saupa's inscrutable face examining her.

King Rencival tilted his head and cocked an eyebrow. "My lady?"

She swallowed and focused her gaze back at him. He smiled encouragingly. "You have gained our attention: you may speak."

Ada drew herself up. "Your Majesty." She scrambled for the right words. "Sire, I cannot speak for both these men, but I know one of them to be a born citizen of your kingdom, and a loyal subject to the crown." Fragments of thoughts pieced themselves together, built from vague nuggets of knowledge she never thought she would need. Her voice grew louder as she gained confidence. "Your noble decrees have commanded that none of your subjects are to be arrested without lawful grounds, and no man condemned without trial. Sire, this man is not a fleeing outlaw. If there is any just cause for his arrest, let it be declared and investigated without this undue cruelty."

As she quoted his own law at him, Rencival's mouth twitched, sliding into a fraction of a smile. But before he could reply, Saupa had barked an enquiry to the Nordish captain. The man swiftly replied and Saupa proclaimed the translation triumphantly. "He is a Burning Heart."

"That is not a crime!" Ada cried.

"Yes, it is!" was the emphatic reply. Saupa looked up, projecting his voice to address the entire court. "Being a Burning Heart is a crime. Maybe not against the civil laws of this land, but it is a crime against nature; against reason and peace; and against the Dragons' Creed. They would overturn any sense of justice and order, treating thieves and murderers as equal with kings. They refuse to pay homage to the dragons and consider it their highest duty to poison others with their same mode of thinking. It has been a plague in our country. Good men have been infected with this madness and lost their minds and wills to it. That is why we have outlawed it, for there can be no secure peace so long as they exist."

Lord Saupa turned to Rencival.

"That is why, Your Majesty, we sought to capture these men before they spread their malice in your land. We requested this both for the peace of your country and our own peace of mind, for we have nothing but goodwill for Your Majesty and your kingdom."

"It is true," spoke Prince Ellis. "Everything my Lord Saupa says is true. We are only grieved to see that the falsehood has already taken root here, even among your own nobles." He looked at Ada.

"I am not a Burning Heart!" she retorted.

"But if being a Burning Heart is nothing to be ashamed of, why would you be indignant that I mistook you for one?"

Ada opened her mouth to answer but could think of no answer, except the one which she could not speak. *But this is Kessler.*

"Enough."

All eyes looked to the king.

"These issues must be discussed, but with proper decorum and with time for just consideration. I appreciate," he continued, forestalling Saupa, "that the matter is urgent. But I fear you will do more harm than good to force the debate now. Come now my lords, let us retire."

As if in afterthought, he motioned his own guards towards the prisoners.

"Take custody of these two but treat them well until this matter is settled."

He nodded a bow to Ada and she curtsied in response. By the time she looked up he had already turned and swept away, his advisors at his heels. It was then that she saw her father for the first time, standing to the left of where the king had been, eyeing her with his level, unreadable expression. He must have been there all along, watching her make a fool of herself in front of the entire court and staying silent, doing nothing to intervene either for her or

Kessler. Her stomach churned but she gave him a respectful obeisance. He turned briskly to join the rest of the council.

Behind her the royal guard were taking charge of the captives. Ada stood back, helpless.

Kessler was more alert, his eyes were open now and glowing, warm with affectionate concern. Ada recognised that look and inwardly moaned. *Kessler you fool. When will you begin to worry about yourself and not me.* How could he be so blind? Her problems would be nothing compared to his if Rencival took against him.

He smiled at her, his whole body gently shedding beams of light. The guards didn't react to it and neither did the crowd. No-one could see the light except her.

Unable to watch anymore, Ada turned away quickly, trying to mingle back into the crowds.

Lord Saupa watched her go.

17

Friend or Foe

Mingling was impossible. Virtually everyone had recognised her during that moment of madness, and those who had not were soon informed. They kept turning to look at her as she passed, murmuring her name. Unable to find a group to slip quietly into, Ada marched on. Yet it was as if everybody was having the same conversation at the same time, so that all the snippets she overheard flowed together into one continuous dialogue.

"I heard of a kitchen maid who was a Burning Heart – they found her drinking her own blood at the new moon."

"Disgusting."

"I think they're more to be pitied than anything. Ambassador Saupa is right: their minds and reason have quite gone. Did you know that they believe that dragons are masters of darkness? What more proof do you need that they are mad?"

"But who would ever have thought that a Dura would be a defender of Burning Hearts."

"Shush, she's right there."

"Shush, don't let her hear you; you don't know how she might react."

"Don't look her in the eye – she might bewitch you."

"Keep away."

"Get away!"

Get *away*?

It was Ada's ears that were burning, not her heart. She had to get out of there. Her gut was twisting tighter and tighter. She was angry but unlike her earlier anger, this sensation was diffused with a fluttering anxiety. Was this what it was like for Iris and Kessler when people found out they were Burning Hearts? Did they face ceaseless whisperings and furtive glances, and the crushing sense of being spurned? She ruefully recalled her own reaction to her discovery about Iris's convictions. Her reactions had been no better, but what did that say about their society when they were all so ready to condemn people they knew nothing about? And in her case, they had got it horribly wrong.

Everyone eyed her like a dangerous animal that might go wild and attack them. One courtier actually recoiled at her approach. Ada sped up. Panic blinkered her vision. After a small eternity, she had broken out of the bulk of the crowd. She burst into a clumsy run.

Don't run, what will everyone think? Ada slowed into a walk.

They already think I'm mad and a Burning Heart. She started forward again.

And you want to confirm their ideas? Ada slowed down.

She was on the verge of starting to run again when, from out of nowhere, Rishard caught her arm, folded it under his own with gentle firmness and escorted her out. Gratitude swelled within her.

When there was no-one close by, Rishard murmured, "That was quite a revelation." His voice lacked the usual humorous bounce. The pressure from his arm no longer felt supportive.

Ada looked up at his face. He continued to face forward, ploughing onwards.

"Rishard?"

He seemed not to hear her and did not speak until they had passed out into the empty hallway. "I didn't know you had that in you," he said in grim quietness.

"Neither did I," she replied.

Her own words stirred up a faint pride. She knew she could be short with servants (as Iris would undoubtedly testify) but to argue with lords and kings...she never thought she would have had the nerve.

He cut through her thoughts. "What were you thinking?"

"They were killing Kessler."

"Don't be silly, he'd only been arrested –"

"'*Only* been arrested'? They had half butchered him already! So don't you dare call me silly. Can't you understand? It was Kessler, *my* Kessler."

"I know, I know." He took a slow breath but didn't speak.

They walked on in silence, still arm in arm but miles apart.

Ada didn't know what she was feeling, but the knot in her stomach had returned and there was a stone in her throat. Why couldn't he understand?

They came out of the great doors and Rishard waved to his grooms to bring the carriage over. Ada realised that he had not even asked her if she intended to leave the castle. Not that she wanted to stay, but for him to assume it was galling.

As the carriage wheeled forward, Rishard pulled her around to face him. "Ada?"

She couldn't quite look into his eyes.

"My love?" He'd never called her that before. It sounded odd, clumsy, wrong. She forced herself to meet his eyes. He looked so...kind. How could he look so kind when he was being so unreasonable?

"I *am* sorry," Rishard said. "More sorry than I can say. I know Kessler is like a second father to you and I know why you did what you did. It was incredible, brave and brilliant. But we can't pretend that it won't change things. Things for us."

She looked at him hard. "For us?"

He hurried on. "I don't want things to change, but I'm afraid that it might after that scene. I only wish you had waited to negotiate Kessler's release in private. I'm just saying this to warn you, just in case..." He trailed off.

Ada was too choked to speak, but she stared at him directly, silently challenging him to meet her eye. He didn't.

The arrival of the carriage broke the awkward pause. Rishard quickly handed her in and closed the door, shutting her in alone. He called instructions to the driver and then he was gone.

Ada stared into the vacant space he had left and kept staring long after the carriage had moved away. She was afraid to think over what Rishard had said, but was incapable of doing anything else. So she sat and looked, cocooned into numbness by shock.

A creeping despair was the first emotion to penetrate. What had she done? She couldn't have left Kessler in the mercy of the Nordish brutes but...but...Her thoughts spiralled in panic. What if Rishard was right and the sensible thing would have been to wait and make private negotiations for Kessler's release? It's what her father would have done. Instead, she had interrupted the King's Council, publicly quarrelled with the ambassadors, implying that they were cruel and unjust and got herself suspected of dragon treason. Far from securing peace with Nordlann she may have destroyed their chances of it.

What had she done?

Things did not calm down when she arrived home: the whole household was in uproar. Ada listened to a dozen voices in a simultaneous, indignant rant about the foreigners' search, incandescently outraged over the arrest of the southern steward and his young guest, and the fact that it had been royally authorised.

Something warm surged through Ada. At least they understood.

Meanwhile the household chamberlain hurried up and barked for silence.

As they quietened down, Ada spoke up, reassuring them that her father knew of Kessler's plight and would doubtless get him released. (She tried to hide her own doubts on the subject.) Then she dismissed them and quickly escaped to her own room.

She felt so tired, so desperately tired. She lay down on her bed. *I just need a little lie down.* Yet before she knew it, she had collapsed into sleep.

Rishard splashed his drink into his throat with careless abandon and leant against the deeply-shadowed wall of the box hedge, feeling thoroughly miserable.

He had been so stupid with Ada, speaking in his social panic and saying far more than he meant. He had probably lost everything as a result, lost her. *What must she think of him?*

Yet why did she have to make a spectacle of herself? No, he knew why and he envied her courage. But he still flushed hot to remember that moment: how those around him had nudged each other, nodded at him and edged away. How long had he been working to ingratiate himself with them? His progress had come on leaps and bounds since the announcement of his engagement to Lord Dura's daughter. Yet with Ada's debacle he had felt himself slipping to the bottom of the pile once again.

All evening he had been greeted with sly references to vixens, shrews and other feisty females. In response he had slipped back to his old methods of self-deprecating laughter and gallant repartee. Only it wasn't self-deprecating; it was Ada he was discrediting. He had been trapped by his own familiar patterns of speech and façade of carefree superiority.

Eventually he had taken refuge in this spot to cool his head and indulge his self-loathing. The still warm evening was diffused with insufferably late sunlight. Would the night never come?

"Why Count Frénore, what a supportive fiancé you are. And what a masterful show of apathy you've treated everyone to." Lady Elina el Rienna transfixed him with a gimlet eye.

It was almost a relief to be finally cornered by her. Every time he tried to laugh off some snide comment about Ada, he had found Lady Elina's eye upon him and had dreaded her witty remarks. At the time he had been grateful for her silence but now she had every appearance of spoiling for a fight. Nevertheless, he bowed courteously. "Ma'am."

She acknowledged the bow and gazed full into his face, unabashed. "Well? What do you have to say for yourself?"

He stared, speechless.

"Come, come. You can't be lost for words *now*. After all, you had plenty to say about your intended bride earlier. Aren't you ashamed of yourself? It has made my blood boil to hear you coolly saying that the poor little girl was naturally upset, but you have sent her home and after some rest she will understand you were right and will see things in their right proportions. The sheer arrogance! Far better to have encouraged her to stay and ride this evening out, though it would have been uncomfortable at first for her – but you are a newly betrothed couple, petted by the king. If anyone had a good chance of being able to distract people from a scene by their sheer status and celebrity, it was you two. It would have shown backbone and you would have both won respect. Instead, just when she's over-exerted herself and needed a good stick to lean on, you go and impale her."

The words came in a soft stream, not loud enough for anyone else to hear, yet Rishard staggered under their blistering force.

Lady Elina didn't wait for a reply but took his arm and sauntered off with him in tow. "Let us see if we can undo the damage you've done. Praise her courage, her outspokenness for justice: speak highly of her like you did to her face at the carriages, *before* you tried to wheedle your way to backing out of your betrothal."

Rishard flushed. "How did you –?"

"Never mind *that*." Her voice was rich with disgust. "It's hardly as important as undoing your mishandled affairs."

She remained limpet-like on his arm as they trailed over the lawn from one group to another, avoiding the various distractions and entertainers that riddled the place. Whenever Ada was mentioned, Rishard felt a slight tightening from Lady Elina's arm and unquestioningly obeyed the silent instruction by expressing his admiration for Ada. To his surprise, once past the initial embarrassment he found himself warming to his task with enthusiasm. Once he even found himself telling his childhood memories of playing with Ada, to which some of the older ladies clucked appreciation and Lady Marguerite il Kishere smiled. At any sign of hostile cynicism to the absent Ada, Lady Elina proved more than a capable ally and when she so displayed her loyalties, no-one dared to engage her in verbal battle.

Finally, they stood alone, all visible worlds conquered, excepting the nearby cluster which included King Rencival and the Lord Saupa.

Lady Elina beamed up at him.

"Now I think we've earned our rest. Would you like..."

She trailed off, gazing with curiosity as Dura interrupted a conversation between the king and Lord Saupa. King Rencival inclined his head without much interest and waved them away. Saupa followed Dura down through the hedge walkway, until the neatly clipped walls of evergreen blocked them completely from view.

"Whatever was that about?" Lady Elina wondered.

"Whatever it was, His Majesty clearly didn't mind being freed from the ambassador's presence."

Certainly, King Rencival was once more talking in his usual animated manner, free from the constraint of his stern Nordlann guest.

An acrobat tumbled and sprung directly in front of them. Keeping them trapped with a rapid succession of flourishing twists and turns before almost as suddenly bounding away to repeat the performance to a different group. As he sprung away, several nobles emerged from the hedged walkway. One of them plodded up to stand alongside Elina, gazing after the retreating acrobat abstractedly.

"Is anything wrong, Lord Rothford?" Elina enquired quietly.

"Hmmm. Not sure if wrong is the right word for it. Peculiar to be sure."

"What was?"

Rishard kept his eyes fixed on the acrobat; afraid the slightest movement would make Rothford clam up.

"Ah, well, not sure I should..."

Elina let him stew in his own silence. Then...

"Oh well," Rothford burst out. "It can hardly be a secret when half a dozen of us overheard it."

"Overheard what?"

"Well," he let out a long snorting breath, "what would you say to Dura and Saupa having a private tête-a-tête?"

"Those two? Really? What about?"

"Well, I didn't hear much. In fact we might not have realised they were in that alcove if Dura hadn't said a little heatedly 'you can't do it tonight!'"

Rishard turned despite himself. Yet the Lord Rothford had now committed to telling his story and continued unperturbed.

"To which Saupa replies something quiet and soothing which we didn't catch, but when Dura repeated 'not tonight' and looked like he was on the point of walking away, Saupa spoke a little louder, 'If it wasn't for your daughter, your steward wouldn't be in the king's dungeon but in my keeping and this complication need not have occurred.' Well...Dura had seen us by then and looked more flustered and angrier than I can remember having ever seen him before. Not a mood to cross him in, so we all carried on up here. Chancellor Elkron was coming towards us; from his face you could see the moment he heard the ruckus and he hurried past us muttering that 'Some people understand nothing about diplomacy!' He's a braver man than I thought to face Dura like that. Anyway, that's all we heard."

They all looked at each other.

"What had to be done tonight?" Rishard asked the air.

"Wouldn't we all like to know," Rothford growled.

18

My Servant from the North

Ada woke.

She remained perfectly still, wondering why she was lying on top of her bedclothes fully dressed. Memories rushed in: Rishard's desertion; running from the muttering crowds; the argument with the Nordish ambassadors; Kessler's beaten body. Kessler!

She jerked upright. Her head spun at the sudden movement. Wincing, Ada kept still, waiting for the dizziness to pass.

The chilly edge of evening air enveloped her, despite the fire someone had lit. *How long had she slept?* Wrapping a shawl around her, Ada got up and closed the shutters. She paused at the last window and looked up at the sky. The moon was low, the sky still luminescent from fading daylight, but the stars were already coming out in twinkling array.

It reminded her of stargazing in Ilnora. Her heart ached. If only she could sit down for a friendly chat where she could express herself freely. She longed to discuss Vlainshai with kindly Guardian Rosquebelle or even tease that old stick

Lady Humber, who would affectionately grumble at her levity. How liberating not to pretend or try to be someone you were not; to be utterly known yet utterly loved. Kessler had loved her like that, or as near like it as was possible for a mortal lantyn. Her recent peevishness against him seemed so petty now.

Ada pushed the regret aside. What could she do now? That was the question. Much as she dreaded the thought, she must speak to her father. She didn't doubt that he would help Kessler, but he would be politically cautious and might leave things too late. Kessler might even now be bleeding to death, in desperate need of a physician, and she had fallen asleep!

The last shutter closed with a bang. She must return to the palace at once, no matter what orders or spies her father may have sent; if she had to she would use the secret passage. There were always other allies she could approach for help, perhaps Lady Elina or even Lady Marguerite.

Yet before she had reached the door it was opened by Iris. The girl's taut face warned of trouble. Ada could guess what that portended.

"Is my father home?"

Iris nodded. "But I believe he means to return to the palace almost at once for the evening banquet. He wishes you to remain at home for the night, and requests that you listen carefully to your visitor."

Someone glided smoothly past Iris. Ada gaped, then remembered her manners and dropped a formal curtsy.

"Ambassador, what a surprise!"

"Please, don't alarm yourself," Lord Saupa said, raising his hands in a pacifying gesture. "I am only here as a friend."

"I'm so pleased to hear that."

Her voice shook a little. This was the man responsible for Kessler's plight, yet could he also be the key to the prophecy? Had the dragons given her a second chance, not only for herself but to free Kessler? Whatever else, she must keep her temper this time.

His mouth slid halfway up one cheek in a crooked smile. "Given the events of earlier today, I am not surprised at your caution and I hope that you will forgive my unpardonable intrusion. I merely seek a private audience and I trust that once I explain, you will believe that my concern for you is both innocent and genuine. Shall we sit?"

Doubt snagged Ada's mind. It didn't feel quite right for Saupa to be in her private quarters, but if her father had arranged this meeting and was waiting downstairs, she supposed it was all right. She sat opposite him on one of the fireside chairs. Yet when Saupa dismissed Iris with an imperious flick of the hand, Ada quickly reinterpreted the movement. "Yes, do shut the door Iris. There's a terrible draught."

Iris nodded, shut the door and stood in front of it, out of Saupa's line of sight.

At least I am not totally alone: Iris is in attendance, father is nearby...With such nagging qualms, it took Ada some time to realise that Saupa had not yet spoken. He sat motionless, staring into the fire.

Restless, she prompted him. "You wished me to hear you out and now you do not speak."

"Forgive me, I only want to make sure I use the right words."

He finally fixed his eyes on her, his soft lilting voice compelling her full attention.

"I understand that your father's steward has been a good friend to you since your early childhood. Seeing him mistreated in any way would prompt your anger, but not everyone would have intervened as you did. As such, I think that your actions today proved that you are a very courageous young woman."

"Thank you," Ada replied, wondering where this was going.

Yet once more he fell silent.

Growing impatient, Ada asked, "If I was right to defend him, why didn't you release him?"

"You still think him harmless. He is not."

"Because he's a Burning Heart?"

He nodded. Ada clenched her fists but took a slow breath. Kessler's fate might depend on this conversation. She adopted a reasoning tone.

"I know they have unusual ideas, but how can we make someone a criminal for what they *think* rather than what they *do*? You said that Burning Hearts bring disorder and chaos, but despite the scandal attached to them they are hard-working and trustworthy."

"It is not what they think that is dangerous; it is what they *are*."

He leant forward.

"Burning Hearts are puppets; lantyns who have fallen prey to a parasitical being of dark magic, disguised as light."

"Light?" Ada echoed. No-one else (Iris excluded) had ever admitted that Burning Hearts were actually indwelt with light. Yet this was a very different portrayal of Yhari.

That one word had betrayed her knowledge. Saupa was staring at her intently, his dark eyes wide.

"You have seen it," he hissed.

His eyes pulled her in. They were deep, black whirlpools, sucking her into their mesmeric depths. Her will was paralysed. He seemed to be looking through her, reading her mind. Suddenly the eyes softened, releasing her from their piercing intensity.

"You have seen," he repeated, his voice now kind, "but you are still free. Most remain blind, with only a dull instinct warning them of danger; it is rare to see. But be warned: seeing Yhari's light can be either very good or very dangerous."

"Why dangerous?"

"Because it means that Yhari hunts you. He seeks to implant you. At first your body senses the danger and recoils, but his masquerade of light appears so beautiful that it lulls you into submission."

Ada's heart thumped hard. He was right. When was the last time she had recoiled from Iris's radiance?

His silk voice glided on. "Once inside it will take over your heart and mind, destroying your individual personality until you are little more than a hollow shell.

As its puppet, the parasite will ensure you live a peaceable life, but you will be only a mindless honey trap used to lure the next victim."

Ada swallowed. Her own arguments defending Burning Hearts as "good people" now only seemed to confirm Saupa's words. Had she been taken in so easily, despite the Oracle's warning against Iris? Yet Saupa had offered a gleam of hope. She plucked at it. "You said it could be good to see this light, why?"

"Because once you can see the trap you can avoid it. However, this places a heavy responsibility on you." His gaze was full of sympathy. "You know now that this threat is real, but to most it is invisible. They think this issue is only a disagreement of ideas and culture, not a reality upon which hangs the fate of the Grey Realm. No, I don't exaggerate: our enemy is one being, able to unite all its individual hosts under its will in a way that no lantyn king ever could. It is steadily conquering the world, country by country and one individual lantyn at a time. The dragons already battle on our behalf but we must do our part. Lady Ada il Dura, will you help me in this fight? Will you serve the dragons alongside me to restore peace and unity."

It was the prophecy. *It was happening, really happening!* For all the solemnity of the moment, Ada felt giddy with relieved triumph. The Oracle had been right. Yet she still didn't really understand what was being asked of her. She had thought the prophecy meant political peace, preventing war between Nordlann and Aven, not battling in a semi-invisible war.

"I serve the dragons as you do," she answered. "But how can we bring peace? How can we free those already implanted?"

Saupa sagged back as if crushed by a heavy weight. "Once the parasite indwells a lantyn the bond is unbreakable."

"Then how can we help them?"

His features twisted into a tortured expression. His eyes tightened in pain.

"We can't. We can only protect those who are not infected by eradicating every possible source of contamination."

Her mind reeled. He couldn't mean what she thought he did.

"Eradicating the sources?"

He met her eye. "We need to kill every Burning Heart as soon as we find them."

Ada felt sick. Following the dragons was supposed to bring life and happiness, not a murderous campaign. Yet everything Saupa said fitted with all the stories she'd heard growing up and even filled in the gaps that the guardians never addressed. Things would be so much simpler if he were right. Part of her even wanted him to be.

And kill Kessler?

Ada looked down at her hands, stomach churning, revolted.

There must be another way to free them of their infection. Yet could she honestly accept that it *was* an infection? A tidal wave of memories with Kessler flooded through her: his comforting her as a child, scolding her for unkindness and praising her for making amends or doing well. Could she really believe that it had all been intended to lull her instincts and lure her into a trap?

She looked up. Her gaze slipped beyond Saupa to Iris. The girl's face was white, yet not surprised; her expression grave yet calm.

Fireworks boomed in the distance; one of the palace celebrations held in the ambassadors' honour. Saupa stood quickly at the sound.

"I have left my duties for too long."

He looked down at her, his voice soft.

"I know you must feel conflicted. What I've described is brutal and ugly work, not something any sane person should enjoy doing, but I am the dragons' servant, and I must do whatever I can to secure peace, not just for Nordlann and Aven but for the world."

Ada nodded mutely and followed him to the door, which Iris opened. Just before he left, Saupa turned to face her once more. He pointed at the silver dragon figurine on her necklace.

"The dragons do not return tribute lightly. Don't delay, secure yourself in their service. Give them your heart. That is the only way to protect it from the great thief. If in doubt, ask them to send the sirens to guide you."

With that, he was gone.

Ada continued to gaze through the empty doorway, frozen in thought. *How had he known her necklace had once been dragon tribute?*

The distant sound of carriage wheels brought her back to her senses. She rushed to the stairs but from the courtyard window she saw that she was too late. Her father's carriage was disappearing through the gate. She had missed that chance to ask him about Kessler's release. Yet after all Saupa had said, was it right to want Kessler released? Although, even if it were, Kessler was probably safer in prison while Saupa was around.

19

The Smoke Charmer's Tale

It was hopeless.

Kelvin slid down to the floor and slumped forwards, head pressing against the bars, gazing at the point where the iron plunged into solid rock. There was no way out of this cage-room without a key to the door.

The air was thick and stifling. Very occasionally the guards passed from their guardroom into this chamber and through a door beyond, or returned the other way. At those moments an almost delicious coolness (which at any other time he would have called dankness) rushed in and made the torch sputter violently in its bracket.

"Kelvin?"

It was Kessler. Kelvin ignored him

"Come here lad and rest properly."

The steward was right of course, he needed to rest and he couldn't stay in this position. His battered limbs were beginning to feel cramped and it was uncomfortable to keep his head half-jammed through the bars. Even so he resented Kessler's advice and kindness. He obeyed as slowly as he could, backing away from the bars and lying down in silence.

The only other prisoner was talking easily with Kessler. They must have taken to each other very quickly, for though their talk was quiet it was – he tried to pin-point the word – enthusiastic. Yes, that was it. There was no other word for it; they were simply and bafflingly, enthusiastic.

Lying shattered and silent, Kelvin felt compelled to listen to the deep voice.

"– and in his goodness, he sent you. I needed the encouragement."

Encouragement? The fool. As if seeing someone joining you in trouble ought to encourage you. And who would send anyone here out of the goodness of their heart?

But Kessler's tone didn't seem the least put out. "And it is a joy to see you again." (*So they did know each other.*) "We couldn't find out what had happened to you after your arrest. Although, for a while, the whole court and city were buzzing about you: the Smoke Charmer who was invited to perform before the king only to spout dragon heresy. They quietly repeated your story of the World's Greying to each other – all the more so when it was known that you were a Burning Heart – but no-one knew what had been done with you. Fynn enquired as much as he dared and all he was told was that your case wasn't being brought to the assizes, but how is that?"

The Smoke Charmer chuckled. "I think Guardian Callum is a little afraid of bringing the case forward."

"Afraid?"

"Yes. Why shouldn't he be afraid? We are servants and actual partakers of his nature, citizens of the conquering kingdom of eternal light. Whenever your tale or my tale finishes here it has only truly begun in the great dawn. Callum serves lizards. They are all doomed to death and destruction, and I think he knows it. He visits every so often and attempts to gloat, but as he is seeking abject fear on my part, he usually leaves in a dissatisfied rage."

"Your courage is wonderful."

"My courage?" The Smoke Charmer's voice was stern. "I shake like a leaf at the thought of those visits; I can feel the heaviness of the dragonish power trying to suffocate me. You and I are nothing by ourselves: it is his light upholding us, and it is impossible to exaggerate the power of Yhari's light. We are nothing yet he is everything. You must grasp that now more than ever." His emphatic voice cracked into a series of thick coughing.

Kelvin winced into the darkness. He hated listening to such sounds.

The Smoke Charmer eventually spoke again, his words broken with ragged breaths.

"Damp...has got...into my lungs. Years of working the smoke don't help...But you haven't...told me...what happened to my apprentices, Gionne...and Fidé?"

"The boys are fine. They were released almost immediately. Gionne was taken up by the Smoke Charmer Alixist, who has apparently long admired his skill and has agreed to continue his apprenticeship. Fidé has joined Brouen at the smithy."

"Good, good," the Smoke Charmer murmured. "Fidé will be happier there. But Gionne was very talented with the smoke shaping. It is good his skill will not be lost, although I wish it were not with Alixist. He is a good teacher, but is hostile to Yhari."

After a long silence Kessler spoke. "I still don't understand how your case has been delayed. But don't tire yourself."

The faint chuckle again. "No, I am better now, thank you. As for my case, I believe Callum fears that King Rencival will be too lenient or even dismiss it, which would create a terrible precedent for others to speak treason against the dragons. Do you know, I sometimes think Callum understands Yhari's power better than most Burning Hearts."

They continued on in this fashion.

Kelvin had long since closed his eyes and maintained the farce of sleep to avoid being dragged into the conversation, although he could have joined in easily. Saupa had been insistent that he learn the Burning Heart's language, but now Kelvin simply wanted to be as far from them as possible.

After a while they began to sing: Kessler's voice hearty; the Smoke Charmer's broken by frequent wheezing bouts.

It was all Kelvin could do not to wrinkle his nose in disgust. *Singing down here, and when in such a state!* Yet he resisted. He would have to watch his thoughts. Thoughts had such a way of showing themselves on one's face. He scarcely dared think about Orla in case his relief at her escape might betray her, and for all he knew Saupa might still be hunting her. Yet while there was still hope for her, his own fate was as good as sealed. He wasn't doomed to endless imprisonment like this Smoke Charmer, or had the hope of release by a friendly master like Kessler. No, he would be handed over to Saupa and he knew what that meant. His only hope was utter and complete recantation of everything to do with Burning Hearts. That wouldn't be a problem: the whole thing had been a ghastly mistake – except for helping Orla.

To think that one moment of weakness should have caused all this; that in return for a slight kindness, he had been told that he had become a Burning Heart. If only he had not listened. If only he hadn't panicked and run. True, he had been far happier among the Burning Hearts than he had ever been with Saupa, but all that nonsense about an invisible light was pure gibberish. They were just as deluded and dogmatic as Saupa, although he knew which regime he would prefer. But there was no choice, there never would be. He had to try and be practical, although it was probably far, far too late for that now.

Would Saupa accept a recantation? That was the pressing question. If he had been a well-known Burning Heart, Saupa would gleefully accept such a plea, but for the protégée who had so embarrassed him...?

Kelvin's heart sank.

A slow grating, scraping sounded.

Kelvin opened his eyes and looked around. The other two had fallen silent at the noise.

All of them caught the gradual movement. Transfixed, they watched the door opposite the guard room entrance.

It swung silently open. A cloaked figure pattered up to the cage and drew back a hood.

Kelvin gazed at the girl. Well, she was a woman not a girl, but there was something childish and gleeful in her face. Those dark crinkles in the crystal skin about the eyes suggested that she was older than her looks, but even so, she was...she was...his mind was spinning in a blank the more he gazed at her.

"Meruda!" Kessler gasped.

Meruda smiled prettily up at him and dimpled at Kelvin. "Yes, master steward," she said. "I've been sent to rescue you."

"Sent? By whom?"

She had already flipped a long pin from her hair and was deftly working at the latch. Two shadows followed her through the door: one remained as sentry, the other came to stand by Meruda's shoulder, a vast sullen and surly shadow. Meruda continued unperturbed by his presence. "Lord Dura of course."

"What?"

"Is that so surprising? He found me and said I could either use my criminal skill for him or enjoy the full penalties of the law for stealing from him. I chose the former."

"But why? My Lord Dura could simply request my release. There is nothing in law to hold me. Why not –"

Meruda made an impatient movement. "It's too late for all that. Saupa has his heart set on that young idiot's blood." She jerked her head at Kelvin. "He's demanded his public execution as part of a peace deal. King Rencival is bound to cave in – Nordlann is on the verge of declaring war as it is.

And by law it will mean your death too since you harboured him. So, unless you want to visit the gallows…" The lock clicked and she opened the door.

"No."

The force of the word took them all aback. Kelvin stared disbelievingly at Kessler's set face. "*If* my master has sent you, I thank him and you. But no, I cannot simply slip away. What damage would this do in law for others? What mischief might result from sneaking away now rather than clearly defending the truth of the matter, even if it does cost me my life? And I'm sorry, but I cannot believe that my Lord Dura would rely on such an underhand method, instead of the open court of law. He is too much a man of principle."

Meruda's eyes shone with tears. "But I cannot bear to see you die so needlessly. You will die if you stay. Please, please." She clutched at his hand. Kessler undid her grasp.

"I must stay," he said quietly. He turned back into the cell.

Meruda darted forward, slipped her arms over Kessler's shoulders and clasped her hands over his face. He writhed mid-air, seized up and fell to the ground.

Meruda recorked a small bottle. Once done, she looked at Kelvin sadly. "He'll thank me one day. I trust we don't need to drug you?"

Kelvin shook his head.

Meruda smiled, then to her giant companion said, "It looks as if we will have to carry the steward out after all."

"We?" the giant muttered as Meruda sped back to the door. All the same, he stepped into the cage.

During the conversation between Kessler and Meruda, the Smoke Charmer had pulled himself upright, one hand clinging to a bar the other clutching his side. As the giant approached Kessler's prone form, the Smoke Charmer opened his mouth to speak.

Those words never came: the giant stabbed him in the chest, wiped the blade on the old man's jacket and proceeded to collect Kessler into his arms.

The Smoke Charmer staggered, his face twisting. Yet in another moment the pain had melted from his face as he gazed, as with delighted recognition, at somewhere beyond the ceiling. Tender warmth embraced the room; shadowy recesses were suddenly visible; an almost unbearable weight of beauty filled the air. The Smoke Charmer flung his arms upwards. His voice rang out: "My Light! My Light!" The very stones of the prison walls resonated with his joy.

The Smoke Charmer rushed forward and left his body behind.

Kelvin blinked through the sudden dimness.

The lifeless form crumpled to the ground.

20

Out!

Kelvin stared at the Smoke Charmer's body, now dead and dark, though the walls still echoed with his jubilant death cry.

A door slammed open. Guards burst in.

The giant shoved Kelvin out of the way and lumbered forward – Kessler still slung over his shoulder – and swung his daggered fist with indiscriminate brute force. Meanwhile, Meruda, who had been nearest to the door, jabbed her arm forward; liquid spurted out in a trail of spray and splashed in the face of the nearest guard. Unlike Kessler, he shrieked as he fell, clutching at his eyes.

The other shadow whirled with lightning jabs.

All motion suddenly ceased. The three turned from their victims to Kelvin.

"Well?" said the giant. "Do you want to join them?" he waved over the scene of destruction pointing with a bloodied blade. "Or us?"

Kelvin flinched as the blade swept towards him. He didn't want to die. He wasn't noble like Kessler. He threw a last look at the crumpled body of the Smoke Charmer.

The sight robbed him of his voice. He obeyed the giant's lead.

They hurried through the door. Meruda shut and relocked it, then hustled them down the passageway.

"Why did you let the old man shout like that?" she snapped at the giant. "Can't you do a simple knifing? Now everyone will know we're here."

"Your own method was a little noisy," the giant muttered. Kelvin thought of the poisoned guard's shrieks and shivered.

Sounds of alarm chased them down the passageway. Feet tramped ahead.

Meruda whisked them down a side passage.

Coolness dripped from the ceiling. The sounds of the plopping splashes danced in echoing circles along the tunnel. The floor grew slippery. The flickering light behind them became a mere suggestion of light. Blackness pressed into Kelvin's eye sockets. Never faltering, his rescuers pressed on and herded him on with them, but they moved at a measured pace: every step threatened to erupt with echoes.

A hand guided him into an invisible right turn. The air felt heavier; all echoes died; quietness pushed into their ears. After a few more moments one of them (Kelvin thought it was the giant) spoke.

"Well, that went well." His voice sounded strange; the oppressive atmosphere half-smothered the words.

"Hush, fool," Meruda said, her voice also clipped short by the acoustics.

"Well, it's plain sailing from 'ere."

"I bet you thought that when you grabbed Lady Ada off the street," said a new, gloomy voice – presumably the third man. "We only had to get her safe out of the way. Quite a simple job really. Laughable the amount he was willing to pay for it and you couldn't even hold onto her."

"Will you fools be quiet and stop announcing our presence to the world," Meruda hissed.

"Come on, it's hardly 'to the world'. Your aristocratic pal there is out for the count and the foreign boy is hardly going to squeal – I'm not sure he can even understand us. I can't see why you're in such a –"

"Shush!" Meruda commanded.

They all froze. Kelvin had heard it too. More than heard: a light flickered ahead. In that pitch black it seemed to blaze out, marking the arched end of their tunnel clearly. A man stood at the entrance holding a torch aloft. The flamelight devoured their masking darkness.

A shout went out. A bustle of movement. Royal guardsmen came flooding down the passageway.

They all ran.

Kelvin stumbled with them. The orange light danced in competition with the utter blackness of their shadows, distorting the sense of the way ahead even more than the complete darkness had.

They turned and were back in the dripping echoes. This time they kept running, not heeding the repeating symphony of clattering footsteps.

Left turn, left turn, right turn, on, on, on. Fleeing from the light and into ever more secure darkness.

Caught in the middle of the group, Kelvin followed their lead, unable to see the ground ahead.

The giant in front halted. Kelvin ran into him, colliding with Kessler's limp form.

They were all standing still. *Why?* They needed to keep moving. He made an impatient step. He tottered on the precipice, flailed against the icy rush of air...and was hauled back.

Gasping, Kelvin rested against the stone wall. His ears pounded too loud to hear any reproofs.

He felt a guiding hand push him forward. He obeyed the direction, trying to feel ahead for one of the others. They were gone; nothing but empty black air. They seemed to have moved away from the wall too. He groped the air, clawing at the void. He shuffled forward, feeling the ground with his toe he found an edge. He held back, uncertain, trying to feel for a step below but it seemed to go down a long way. His guide grew impatient and the pressure increased to a push. Kelvin rocked forward and found the ledge of the step. The steps went on.

A tiny light sputtered into existence.

Kelvin could now see that they were descending to something like a jetty. Dark greenish water gurgled past, sucking and pulling at everything and nudging at the tethered skiff which bobbed ahead.

The giant placed a lolling Kessler in the stern and himself stepped in at the bow. He reached for a chain which looped through a great metal ring sticking out from the jetty's corner post. As he lifted it up from the water, Kelvin saw that the chain also looped through a ring at the skiff's prow and stretched along the wall to the left of the jetty. The giant began to haul and from the jetty Meruda hauled too. Tugged by the chain, the boat edged upstream along the water-way to the left, disappearing behind the corner.

Meruda looked up at Kelvin and the remaining man angrily, sweat beading her flushed forehead. "Are you going to help or what? He's no lightweight."

"Sorry," muttered the other and set to. Kelvin joined in. Coil after coil of the wet and sometimes slimy chain passed through their fingers. After what felt like a year there was clanking and a great knot in the chain clanked against the loop.

"Good he's got there. We'll wait for him to start pulling the other way," Meruda gasped.

Kelvin sat back on the step, his head swimming. He felt himself shaking. It had been many hours since that one good meal back at the Dura mansion and the weeks before that food had been scanty at best. He thought longingly of the stew Kessler had given him, yet to his surprise the thought of food made him feel sick. He leant forward letting the cool air rush over him. Every little discomfort seemed to intensify, each demanding attention: the bruises Saupa's men had given; the stench of the gurgling green water; his throbbing head...He shut his eyes and inhaled deeply through his mouth.

He heard the others talking, keeping their voices soft.

"Shouldn't we put the light out?"

"No. We'll only have to light it again to get in the boat."

"What was going on back there with the torch-man? Who was he?"

"Sniffer," Meruda spat.

"Who?"

"You know, the one who interrupted you in the tunnels last time."

"Oh *him*. I wouldn't mind meeting him again. I owe him a black eye and one or two other things."

"Well let's hope you don't get the chance tonight."

"What's he doing here anyway?"

"He'll be after Dura's steward."

"What? Same as us? Who does he work for? Those were royal guardsman he had with him!"

"Anyone might hoodwink a few guardsmen for their own purposes. As to masters, we probably share the same one."

"Then why does he keep working against us and getting in the way?"

"Stop asking stupid questions. He wants the credit and payment all for himself. Look, the chain's moving again. Quick, pull the boat back."

Kelvin thought about moving but the very idea of getting up made him dizzy.

"Oi, lazybones, are you going to help?" the man called.

"Leave him be," Meruda grunted.

Kelvin listened in grateful stillness. He heard the slapping water, the chain's final clank, the shouts and rapid tramp of boots.

"*Quick*."

He felt himself bustled up. Kelvin opened his eyes and helped them as best he could to step and slump into the boat. The others nimbly leapt in and began hauling at the chain, pulling the boat along the wall of the water-way and out of sight of the steps.

The voices and steps erupted in volume: their pursuers had entered the jetty chamber.

Meruda gesticulated silently. The man leapt out of the boat and up into a small alcove in the wall. Kelvin tried to follow, but his limbs had run out of strength. The water rushed up to meet him. Someone's hand caught him and hauled him up. A moment later he was pressed against the stone and Meruda sprang up to join them. They all leant back as far as possible, hiding out of sight.

A new bright light reached around the corner from the jetty. It illuminated the greenish tinge of the dark waters; lit a skulking rat on the far side of the water channel; it showed the empty skiff, bobbing irritably against the current. The light did not move but stayed in place as if watching, thinking.

The voices of men echoed in a confused medley. Eventually, there was some order, and the boat was hauled back to the jetty.

For the first time Kelvin felt Meruda's breath quicken. He heard the man's whisper, scarcely more than mouthing. "If they take the ferry along here ..."

They waited, expecting to hear the chain clank then see the boat edge into view below them filled with guardsman. None came. Instead, there was a hurried patter of feet, more voices; then the bright light retreated, leaving the small distant glow. The quick tramp of feet faded into silence.

"*Now*," Meruda breathed. She and her companion squatted down, reached for the chain and eased the skiff back towards them.

Kelvin clung to a jutting stone, desperate not to swoon and drop into the water. In a daze he let them guide him back into the boat and felt it recommence its jerky progress.

Soon afterward, the air changed into a cool fresh breeze. All at once they were out, under the still luminous blue of a midsummer night sky, dotted with early stars. He heard the distant boom and crackle of fireworks.

Another light – a lantern held by the giant – swayed over them. They were tugging him up onto solid ground, but then Kelvin found his arms being twisted behind him. Rough rope bit around his wrists. Coarse strips of material were shoved into his mouth and covered by a final gag. He struggled, but it was hopeless. They laughed at his feeble efforts until he gave up and slumped in exhaustion. Numb despair lullabied him into darkness.

The next few hours were a confused jumble. Between bouts of blacking out, he felt himself bundled along. It was like a never-ending, restless dream Why didn't they leave him be?

Finally they stopped and he was dropped against a stone wall. He let his head sag forwards with his eyes closed. Above him their voices congratulated each other.

"This has been a good night's work." Meruda's voice brimmed with satisfaction. "Dura's steward safely out of the way and we have Saupa's runaway."

"I'm very glad to hear it."

Kelvin's heart stopped. He knew that voice.

He could tell from the quick shuffle of feet that the others had been surprised too, yet Meruda's voice answered smoothly enough. "My Lord Saupa, as requested: one runaway scribe."

A pair of hands gently removed the gagging and lifted Kelvin's head.

Saupa was squatting in front of him. His eyes held Kelvin.

"Where is the girl?" Saupa spoke in Nordish, his voice soft. "The one you travelled with?"

Orla! Kelvin closed his mouth.

Saupa nodded. "I see."

Pain erupted in Kelvin's chest. Before it reached its full agony, another fireball exploded in his shoulder, the other elbow, his knee and half a dozen points in his body. He couldn't even scream; his breath had been driven out.

The pain subsided. Gasping, his vision blurred, Kelvin felt himself being righted, a pair of hands on his shoulders, locking him in place. As his sight refocused, he met his old master's eyes. They were hard yet appraising.

"You were such a good student; it's surprising your treachery should fail so dismally. You haven't warned the Avenese court, you've led me to other dragon traitors and for a so-called Burning Heart, you don't so much as glimmer. There's hope for you, perhaps."

Saupa cocked his head on one side.

"Where is the girl?"

Something clicked in Kelvin's brain. He knew Saupa well enough to know that he wasn't playing with him. If he was asking like this, Saupa really didn't have a clue where to find Orla or was too short of time to search properly. He was cut off from his normal resources and was panicking.

Triumph surged through Kelvin. He had won. He would win. He didn't care about all his other failures, but the one important thing was Orla's safety. Saupa had not found her and he would not. He only had to resist for a short while, enduring whatever pain Saupa inflicted, and Orla would be free and safe with those who would care for her.

The mad joy showed on his face. Saupa bared his teeth.

A fresh firework display began to thunder in the distance.

Saupa flicked his head in annoyance.

"Time's up," he said.

His fist flashed towards Kelvin's head.

The world went dark.

21

On the Way Home

After the sultry afternoon, the rush of cool air was a relief.

Rishard spurred his horse, determined to keep up with Elina's carriage, which drove at a reckless speed only possible in the empty night streets of a respectable neighbourhood. Muffled curses and complaints from drowsy households were thrown after them, but were largely drowned by the clattering hooves, rattling wheels, and the resounding booms of fireworks.

A short while ago, Elina had insisted that he ought to get Ada a present to apologise.

"But I can't buy her favour."

Elina's eye had twinkled at his doubtful tone. "Good, you're learning. But while everyone protests that gifts don't sway them, nearly everyone is pleased to receive them. Ada's not that much of a curmudgeon, but you'll still need to give her something very special as a peace offering."

"Very special?" Rishard had echoed, his mind blank.

Elina chuckled. "You're hopeless. However, I have just the thing. I knew Ada's mother quite well and I still have something that belonged to her. Lord Dura isn't one to cling on to trinkets, so such a gift would be precious to Ada. I am quite willing to sacrifice it for the sake of young love."

Rishard shuffled, flushing. "You are most kind."

"Well let's slip away from the festivities and if you escort me home, I'll find the token and you can give it to Ada first thing tomorrow."

"Escort you home? But surely you live here in the palace. You are the female head of the royal family, in fact, you're the only royal lady."

"True, but I have property elsewhere in the city, and when the palace gets clogged up with visiting nobility and foreign dignitaries, I prefer to transfer my residence."

Although pleased to have Lady Elina as an ally, Rishard had doubted the propriety of escorting her to her private home. He would have refused if it hadn't been for Lady Marguerite's approval (that most respectable of all ladies) and her pointing out that with the accompanying groom and coachman, he need never be alone with Elina.

So it was that as the fireworks began, Elina's carriage wheeled out of the palace gates with Rishard and a groom following on horses from the royal stable.

Elina's private residence proved to be some distance from Vière Castle: the fireworks had long finished and still they rode at speed. Rishard wished they had waited until morning when the populace would have forced a more sedate pace. He was tired and navigating cobbles on a strange horse, even in strong moonlight, demanded concentration.

A quick movement, somewhere high to his left, caught his eye.

The coachman yelled; the carriage horses screamed as they crashed to their knees. The carriage flew forward, smashed into the horses, sending the driver flying over them and the carriage body skidding off to the right. It slammed into a house. Dust and splinters erupted into the air.

Rishard pulled his reins hard left. His mare swerved from the collision and bolted down a side-alley. He felt the animal's panic and let the reins go slack, trying to radiate calmness to the creature. Yet he felt alarmed at the growing distance between himself and the crash. He was only glad the narrow confines of the alley were free from pedestrians at this late hour.

The central fountain of an open square gleamed ahead. As they emerged, Rishard pulled one rein gently. The horse circled the space, slowing and snorting. Rishard patted its neck, murmuring soothing phrases. As it calmed, he directed it to the fountain. Keeping up the flow of reassurances, Rishard dismounted and swiftly tied the bridle to a ring on the fountain rim, then sprinted back the way they had come.

He dared not trust that horse to return to the fray. It would have been different if it had been his own steed, trained to cope with flashing steel and battle conditions, but this nervous beast was best left behind.

Running felt so slow after that wild gallop. He pumped his arms and legs. *Run faster can't you?* He willed himself on, dreading that he might be too late to help.

He shot out of the alley.

Two men were attacking the groom. Another was at the carriage door beyond.

The groom was felled. His assassins turned on Rishard.

Rishard threw himself on the nearest, gripping the man's waist and using his own momentum to twist and throw him. The man crashed down and lay still, stunned or worse. The other jabbed forward with a knife. Rishard sidestepped, caught the wrist and yanked it hard. His assailant howled and the knife fell with a clatter. Rishard headbutted him and he crumpled up.

Rishard started to the carriage and halted.

Elina stood by the wreckage, her head on one side as she watched him, great loops of hair drooping over one shoulder. The last attacker already lay limp and lifeless at her feet. She finished wiping a long and vicious-looking hair pin, twisted her loosened tresses up and slotted the hair pin back in place.

With only a nod, she hurried to the coachman who lay senseless beyond the screaming horses. Following her example, Rishard stooped down to examine the groom but quickly saw that there was no hope. The assailants he had dealt with had been more fortunate. He quickly felt for and removed their various weapons.

Shouts rang out, ordering him to stand still. The Watch had arrived and were running towards him.

Nothing loath, Rishard obeyed. Once they were nearer and saw his clothes, they seemed to reassess their attitude. Rishard pressed home the advantage and overrode their questions.

"Secure these fellows: they assaulted Lady Elina el Rienna's transport and have killed her groom and another of her men lies injured over there. Someone find a physician."

He hurried over to Elina who knelt by the coachman. He was still breathing.

In windows all along the street, shutters were opened and lights appeared. People emerged, voicing curiosity and shock. Someone with a hastily thrown on coat rushed out and joined the gathering around the coachman. He called orders to a child in a nearby doorway who disappeared and soon returned with the demanded items.

Lady Elina let Rishard help her up and out of the way, although she winced at the movement and clutched at the back of her neck. She ignored all expressions of concern and advice; the only concession she allowed herself was to cling to Rishard's arm as she stepped purposefully back up the street.

They passed by the horses. The creatures still flailed between the carriage shafts, unable to get up. Their legs were broken. Rishard looked to Elina. Her face was white with pity and anger but she nodded. Rishard gave the order and a guard put the horses out of their misery. Elina shuddered at their sudden silence.

It was then that Rishard saw the rope. It trailed across the cobbles, stretching over the width of the street and under the horses' bodies. The end nearest them was still tied around a wooden post, which had been uprooted by the force of the collision; the other end was tied to a metal ring fixed into the stone wall. Elina saw it too.

She hissed, "Someone will pay for this." She let go of Rishard's arm and stalked towards the two surviving assailants.

Before she reached them one of the Watch stepped forward. "Excuse me sir, we found a horse tied up around the corner and –"

"Oh, yes. The animal bolted in a panic. I managed to partially calm it but tied it up out of the way. If it's quiet now you could bring it back before someone steals it."

The man hurried off.

Elina had stopped to stare down at the groom's body. "How am I meant to tell his mother? Or tell Jacqueline about her husband? They were good servants and deserved better. Whoever did this..." Her voice choked. She did not cry. Not a single tear threatened to moisten her eye, but avenging fury imprinted every line.

A clip-clop of hooves approached. Rishard turned to the sound, only to freeze, gaping. "But that's..." He couldn't finish. It was not the horse he had ridden earlier. This was a large black stallion with a white splash mark over the right fore-knee. It was Dester, Dura's personal horse.

Elina recognised it too. Shock replaced all other emotion. "I can't believe it."

A sudden thought struck Rishard. He pounced forward to the two prisoners and examined their faces. He drew back grimly. "I recognise him," he said, pointing at one of them. "He attended my horse when I visited Ada. He works for Dura."

22

Arrest

Something collided with Ada from behind, sending her staggering. A ball rolled past her and thumped against the wall.

"Orla!"

Ada heard Iris's cry and was aware of her maid hurrying down the hallway, but she only had eyes for the child who had run into her. The girl looked up from beneath loose strands of gleaming hair, her brow wrinkled in shy apology. Ada swallowed. The resemblance was uncanny: she was staring into a face she had thought long lost to the grave. The child was even wearing one of Niadre's dresses. The foggy memory of her little sister's face melted away, eclipsed and supplanted by the one before her.

Ada returned the smile, her heartstrings twisting. She stooped for the ball and offered it back. The girl took the ball, but when Iris joined them, she quickly shrank back into the maid's skirt.

"You shouldn't have run out like that," Iris chided in a rush.

Orla looked up at her, penitence written on her face, and answered in a pretty but unintelligible jabber. Nordish. Ada recognised the sound if not the words and tingled in anger. This was Saupa's doing. This homeless child and her imprisoned keeper were the fruit of his handiwork. He had pursued them here and taken Kessler. She suddenly wondered why they had come here. Had it been mere chance?

"My lady, could we go somewhere more private?" Iris glanced nervously up and down the passageway.

Ada hesitated. For all her anger at Saupa, was he right? Was it safe to be with Iris, a Burning Heart? Yet without his compelling presence, his arguments now seemed outrageously extreme. Ada looked down at Orla and softened. She was so young.

Together they returned in silence to Ada's rooms.

Orla peeped out at Ada with a cautious smile and tossed the ball up to her. An impromptu game of catch ensued, and Orla's ready giggles and chatter coaxed smiles from them both. Iris told the tale of Orla's bath and bravado during the manhunt, eliciting fresh mirth. Orla looked puzzled at their laughter, but decided to join in with gusto. Yet after a while, her smile faded and she looked up at Iris.

"Kelvy?" she pleaded.

Iris picked her up, rocked her back and forth and spoke soothingly, explaining that Kelvin had gone for now, but that she would look after Orla. The girl couldn't understand Avenese, and repeatedly asked for Kelvy with growing distress, her face puckered up.

Ada watched, deeply uncomfortable. For once she was glad to be totally ignored and to have Iris dealing with the situation.

Orla's cries threatened to break into a wail. Iris firmly moved the girl so that they were face to face. She then patted her heart and patted over Orla's, closed her eyes and began to talk quietly. Orla fell silent.

Reality flickered. Ada braced herself, but this time the light was not reaching for her with its painful grasp. Instead, the golden light not only radiated from both Iris and Orla, but the beams reached out to embrace the girls, swathing them in a hug of light.

"O Yhari, we're scared for Kelvy and Master Kessler," Iris said simply. "We don't know where they are, but you know and you are with them. Thank you. Thank you that you are with us too. Help us to remember that." She continued in the same vein for some time.

Fascinated, Ada watched, listened and brooded. From the little she could see of Orla's face, it was screwed up tight in concentration. Yet if Orla didn't speak Avenese, how could she know what was going on? Did communing with Yhari surpass spoken languages? Saupa had said that Yhari united Burning Hearts in a unique way. Yet he had also said they were mindless puppets; in which case, why would Iris need or want to talk to Yhari? Was this all a trick?

After a while, Orla snuggled against Iris and lay still.

Ada eyed them. Even amid trouble they seemed so content and confident in being loved; the picture of peace. Longing and bitterness gnawed at her.

"How do you know what is real?" The question slipped out without her thinking.

Iris smiled. "I'm not a philosopher, my lady."

"That hasn't stopped you before. How can I know whether to trust the dragons or Yhari?"

Iris cocked her head. "Why do you ask, my lady?"

"Why? Because it changes everything. I've always believed in the dragons and the world made sense. I believed the Oracle's prophecy, but if Saupa is right, where will it lead? Whereas Yhari –" Ada stopped, tangled in her own thoughts. She had spoken as if she no longer believed the Oracle's prophecy, but she did, didn't she?

Iris waited a long moment before prompting. "Whereas Yhari?"

Ada pulled herself together. "It's too good to be true. The happy contentment, the peace, the patience, it's all an act. It can't be real. After all, how can it? To have that light burning permanently within you must be endless agony."

"Once it was agony," Iris agreed, stroking Orla's head. "I was a creature of darkness. Yhari is purest light and he showed me myself. I hated him for that and fought the synaiad he had given me, ignoring the truth it spoke, determined to be my own light. Yet the more I resisted him the darker my heart became."

Ada couldn't help but be angry on Iris's behalf. *Who had so distorted the girl's thinking?*

"Fighting for your identity doesn't make you some darkened monster!" she protested.

Iris gave her a strange look. "But, my lady, Yhari is light. To reject him, to not accept him, is to choose darkness. It was only when I submitted to Yhari that I could shine, and truly be who I was meant to be. Now his presence is an increasing delight, although my body is still tainted by the dark disease, but on the final victory day, I will be utterly transformed in immortal light."

Ada wished she hadn't started the conversation.

"A pretty piece of moonshine," she answered, striving to keep her voice light. "But if it were that good, surely everyone would accept his light?"

"*Light has come into the world, and people loved the darkness rather than the light, because their deeds were evil. For everyone who practices evil hates the light and does not come to the light lest his deeds be exposed,*" Iris quoted softly.

Ada shivered. They were the very words *The Light Lore* had seared into her, making her appear like a wizened husk in its mirrorstone. How had Iris known to quote that? It was unnatural.

"My lady," Iris began, "much of what Lord Saupa told you was true but twisted. He –"

Ada started up. She stormed out of the room and down the corridor, ignoring the calls Iris made after her. She couldn't listen anymore. She padded along the hallway, trying to clear her mind. Saupa and Iris. How could two such opposing ideologies both pull at her? There was a compelling power to each, yet neither could be completely right, and in certain regards both of them seemed mad.

Thud. Thud. Thud. An unseen voice demanded entry.

Ada looked down into the courtyard and saw the doorman hasten to the gates. After checking the hatch, he hurried to the main door. The moment he opened it, a flood of royal guardsmen pushed past him. They divided into units and streamed towards the various entrances to the building.

Ada flew back to the bedroom. "The manhunt's returned," she announced. "We need to get Orla out of here. The front entrances are guarded: let's check the back."

Iris started up, clutching Orla, and together they slipped to the window and peeked through the shutter slats towards the garden gate. The brilliant moonlight showed the men already standing guard there.

"Is there any other way out?" Iris asked.

"Yes." Ada scurried back to the door. "Follow me." She headed for the bird tower.

They ran lightly on tiptoes, down the moonlit corridor, dreading each creaking floorboard, yet not daring to go slowly or look back. The invaders' noise closed in from behind and ahead.

It wasn't far. Ada yanked the tower door open. It creaked with a mighty groan. They hurried in and Ada drew the bolt. All was black.

Orla whimpered. Iris hushed her as she and Ada felt their way up the stairs. After the first turn, moonlight reached down from the windows above to aid their climb. As they reached the top, someone tried the door below. The wood creaked in protest. Someone shouted an order but the words were muffled.

Ada flew to the secret door and worked it open. Iris crept in and Ada passed Orla through to her.

"Follow the passage," Ada said quickly. "It'll lead you to a drain entrance on the street. Get her somewhere safe. Here." She thrust forward a purse of coins she had seized on her way out of the bedroom and closed the door on the two white faces.

The wooden doorframe below splintered. Shouts rang suddenly loud and clear. Footsteps pounded up the stairs. Ada stepped over to the far window, brushing dust off her skirt. She turned, feigning shock as the guardsmen poured in.

"What is the meaning of this?" she demanded.

"The real question is why are you skulking up here?" returned the captain of the group.

"How dare you talk to me like that! Who are you? What gives you the right to ask me what I do in my own home?"

He stepped into the patch of moonlight and tapped the insignia on his chest. "His Majesty's royal decree that we detain you."

"Detain *me*?" Ada stared. "Whatever for?"

"It's all right Captain."

The men parted. Chancellor Elkron stepped forward between them and bowed. "Lady Ada, my apologies for such an intrusion, but it is essential. Where is your father?"

"He returned to the palace some time ago," Ada answered, even more bewildered. "What is going on?"

Chancellor Elkron did not answer but peered with interest through the gloom towards the aviary. He called for a light.

Ada gasped. The cage was empty. The birds had gone.

"Dura's famous messenger pigeons," Elkron murmured. He turned back to Ada. "What were you doing up here Lady Ada?"

"I like to come here. It's free of busybodies. At least it *was*."

"And during your moonlight contemplations up in this eyrie tonight, you didn't happen to notice that the birds were missing?"

"If I had, I would have told someone; my father prizes them."

"Indeed. You didn't let them out yourself?"

"I just said my father prized them. I wouldn't dare. Now tell me what is going on?"

Elkron didn't answer. He walked past her to peer out of the window, then repeated the action at the other. He shrugged to himself and signalled the men to escort her downstairs.

They took her to her father's strong room. The household chamberlain stood by the open door, no longer superior nor obsequious, but shuffling from foot to foot as he fingered the door key, his brow gleaming with sweat. He flushed at the sight of Ada but stood aside for Chancellor Elkron.

Elkron began to search, swiftly sorting through papers, trying drawers, demanding access to any locked chest. Eventually he picked out a document, frowned and turned to Ada. "Do you know Sir Deln?"

Ada blinked. "I believe he's a gentleman with lands near Trienne."

"Which border your father's estates."

"Yes, somewhere to the northwest end of my father's lands, but I don't know him personally. I've always lived in Ilnora in the far south."

"Does your father often correspond with Sir Deln?"

"I don't know."

The chancellor delicately sliced the wax seal open. Ada bit back her indignation at the intrusion, yet she was curious: sealed letters were for immediate dispatch, not for storing in a strong room.

Elkron's frown deepened as he read. He passed the paper to Ada. "Do you have any explanation?"

Ada ran her eye over the document. The handwriting was not her father's, but that meant nothing; a scribe might have written it at his dictation. More importantly, the wax was imprinted with the Dura crest, a winding river under a pacing lion. It was the seal of his signet ring. He had officially approved whatever this letter said.

She began to read. It contained details of a journey that Lady Elina el Rienna was due to make near Trienne, and gave instructions to Sir Deln to abduct Elina. He was then to convey her to the Dura valley, where Lord Dura would forcibly marry her.

Ada closed her eyes as she absorbed the implications. Her father had always impressed upon her the importance of their lineage; how they shared an ancestor with Rencival, King Fisk the Savage. If he married Elina, the only woman of full royal blood, he would have a strong claim to the throne and with his immense resources of lands and wealth, Rencival's overthrow would be a matter of time. But her father had always been the epitome of loyalty. He couldn't have done this.

"You have no explanation?" Elkron enquired.

"Why should I have an explanation?" Ada flared back. "I don't know anything about this. But my father has the greatest respect for the Lady Elina, he wouldn't plan or be a part of anything so treasonous. And I ask you: does it make sense that my father would write such a letter, seal it and *not* send it?"

"Whereas you suppose that someone forged the letter and seal, broke into this strongroom, planted this letter and relocked the door without discovery – all without stealing the smallest trinket for their trouble. Is *that* likely?"

Ada opened her mouth and froze. Meruda had been caught working at the strongroom's lock. Yet since nothing was missing, it had been assumed that she had failed to get inside. But what if she had already been inside? Could Meruda have done this? The thought was staggering.

"While it would have been more prudent to destroy this letter," Elkron continued, "no-one is immune to mistakes, especially when rushed. And we know that Dura's co-conspirator pressurised him to change his plans at short-notice – there are multiple witnesses to that conversation. In fact, this letter is also evidence not only of Dura's guilt, but that his plans changed, as he attempted to abduct Lady Elina earlier tonight. The attempt failed."

Ada sat down heavily. "Where is my father now? What does he say to all this?"

"Lord Dura disappeared tonight, shortly after a private conference with Lord Saupa, which your household chamberlain overheard. Tell her."

The chamberlain wouldn't meet Ada's gaze but stared down at his feet.

"When the master returned with Lord Saupa – just before Lord Saupa came in to you, my lady – they remained in the carriage a short while talking. They didn't realise I was so close: I heard the Nordlannder promise your father military aid to overthrow His Majesty King Rencival."

Ada blinked. "But what of the peace negotiations?"

Elkron waved the question away impatiently. "They never had interest in the talks! The Nordish delegation departed some time ago, before this incident was reported. As soon as Saupa had returned alone, his fellow ambassador, Prince Ellis, began his tantrum, declaring that they had been insulted – your earlier public spat was the prime reason given. They were gone within the hour; their servants were already prepared to leave. The whole thing was a front and now we know why. As such," Elkron concluded, "Lord Dura is wanted on a charge of high treason. You, Lady Ada, will be detained in your rooms until you are wanted for further questioning."

23

Trapped

Shafts of sunlight streamed in from between the shutter slats. Through half-lidded eyes, Ada regarded the slanting rays. It was morning.

Morning? She bolted up and winced, stiff from sleeping in a chair. Elkron had not returned with his questions; she must have dozed off while waiting for him.

As she rotated her neck, trying to loosen it, Ada noticed that her wash basin had been refilled and a tray of food and drink placed on the side table. There was nothing luxurious in the choice of viands but the quantities were generous. Evidently, they were going to make her wait a bit longer.

The room felt stuffy. Ada hobbled to the windows and flung back the shutters. Birdsong, mingled with the noise of the bustling city, rushed to her ears. It dawned on her that the house was filled with an unnerving stillness. No servants going back and forth cleaning the rooms, setting fires and making beds, instead, silence.

Something scuffled below. Two housemaids were scurrying out to the garden gate, where a royal guardsman stood sentry. Ada called to them. One girl looked up, but her companion pulled her on. The guard let them pass and they disappeared.

The sunshine lost its warmth.

Ada suddenly longed for Iris and rang for her.

Minutes passed.

No Iris appeared. In the circumstances perhaps that wasn't surprising, but the sense of loneliness overwhelmed her. She went to the door. As she had expected, it was still locked, but she caught a stir of movement and the faint murmur of voices beyond.

"Hello?" Both movement and murmur ceased. "I want to speak to Chancellor Elkron."

No response. She banged on the door and repeated the request. This time there was a laugh and the hum of conversation continued.

Ada retreated, flushing hot. She resolved not to try the door again, or call to its sentries. She wouldn't give them any reason to laugh at her. She was a Dura after all. A Dura. What did that mean now? Her very name was a disgrace. Even the servants didn't want to associate with her. But let them shy away or laugh, she would show them! When they came for her, she would look the part. She chose her most elaborate ball gown and tried to change into it by herself. She quickly regretted the choice.

"Someone...definitely...needs to...invent...better clothes," Ada muttered while wrestling and contorting to conquer the lace-up fastenings down her back with no Iris to help. Eventually she was satisfied that she was more or less presentable.

Now for styling the hair...She thoughtfully considered the array of torture instruments and decided to simply brush her hair through.

Then the waiting began in earnest. Soon she was pacing.

Rishard, Kessler, Iris, Orla, Father, Saupa...their names bounced around her skull with each step and each turn twisted her gut into a fresh knot.

She ran over the evidences against her father. Whatever Elkron might say, the sloppiness of leaving an incriminating letter to be found, and of plotting within earshot of others, did not fit with her father's meticulous character. Others must be framing him. The chamberlain had to be involved and, probably, Meruda.

Meruda's betrayal was a difficult idea to stomach, but she had to be honest. After all, beneath Meruda's vivacious friendliness, how well did she know her? Her service had lasted six months; Iris's a few weeks; yet Ada was confident that she knew more of Iris's deepest character than she did of Meruda's.

The attempted abduction of Lady Elina was harder to argue away. Ada wished she knew more. Her helpless ignorance was infuriating.

On top of that, why had her father disappeared if he were innocent? And if he were guilty, had he considered her of such little importance as to leave her behind? He could have at least staged her kidnapping.

Ada's stomach dropped. Memories rushed back to her. Gigantic hands dragging her away from the sunlight. The cold dank air of the waterway tunnels. Struggling for breath in the dark. Someone *had* tried to kidnap her, almost immediately upon her arrival in Casida, before she even knew of the betrothal. If her father had arranged that, had he even intended her to become formally engaged to Rishard, or could that be another device to distance himself from likely blame?

If her father was deemed guilty, what would that mean for her? Ada stopped short. They would condemn her too. Coldness gripped her. She had never witnessed an execution for high treason, but the accounts were ugly. She collapsed into a chair. For a long time, all she could do was sit there, her thoughts numbed, rubbing her shaking arms, hands and fingers as if to reassure herself that her body was still whole.

The shadows grew long.

Her tummy rumbled a complaint. Her head ached.

Ada glanced at the food, feeling sick. Despite what she felt, she knew she ought to try to eat and drink. She experimented cautiously. She quickly felt better. Besides, the act of doing something was a relief. She took her time, nibbling her way through the supplies. It became a game of seeing how slowly she could eat; anything, rather than thinking.

As the shadows lengthened into darkness, Ada finally resigned herself to the fact that no-one was going to visit or release her that day. Should she undress? After the struggle of getting into the monster ball gown, she was severely tempted to simply sleep in it. Yet the heinous crime proved beyond her and she began the painful process of undressing. At least it passed the time and tired her out.

No-one came the next day, nor the next.

Each day her appreciation for Iris grew. Ada grew desperate for a proper bath and dreamed of luxuriating in a large bathtub; despite her best efforts with the wash basin, her hair felt itchy with grime.

Yet the itch in her mind was worse.

Her world's foundations were crumbling. Everything she had clung to or hoped for had turned on its head and proven hollow: her family name, position, Rishard, and as for the destiny the Oracle promised – that last one was a cruel joke, as working with Saupa apparently meant the betrayal and invasion of her homeland and the slaughter of those who had only ever shown her kindness. It was the opposite to peace. Yet it was unthinkable that the dragons were mistaken, or worse.

Ada had been staring blankly into the distance, but now she realised that she was facing the bookshelf, looking directly at *The Light Lore*. It was supposedly the dragons' gift to lantyns, provided only the dragnoss guardians read it, yet it was in its pages that she had seen Yhari. She remembered her own experience of reading *The Light Lore* and how Yhari had tried to make her think that she was a monster. Ada shuddered. What a horrible lie.

"You know it was true."

Ada started. Sitting next to her, laying a hand on her shoulder was...herself? There was another Ada, but it was not quite solid and it stared so very gravely. Ada doubted that her face had ever looked quite so solemn. The phantom, or whatever it was, stared hard.

Ada gasped in shock. Her mind was being held in a vice-like grip; her thoughts dragged back to the memory of her reflection in *The Light Lore*. Ada struggled but the image ballooned to fill her entire mental vision. She was a withered husk of darkness.

No, *no*, *no*! It was all a trick. Saupa had warned her. It was part of the illusion to make her want the parasite.

Still the phantom stared, boring into Ada's mind.

More memories forced their way to the surface: Iris and Kessler glowing; all the discrepancies Ada had witnessed between the guardians' teachings and *The Light Lore*; Iris speaking of Yhari. Her whole life began passing before her. Only now she saw herself darken and wither with every spiteful thought, each irritable word and the selfish motivation in even her kindest moments. In each passing memory, she saw herself grow yet darker and more hideous.

Ada felt sick. Her insides had been chewed into mush by guilt. And still that heavy force pressed on her mind, weighing her down with the wordless conviction that it was telling her the truth.

How am I supposed to fight this? She glared defiantly back at the stern phantom. "Whatever you are, doing stop it."

It continued to stare accusingly.

"Don't believe her; that isn't you."

Ada whirled towards the new voice. Kneeling before her was a beautiful creature. Its body seemed to be made of solidified blue mist, with a soft glow which mysteriously emitted a sense of comfort and familiarity. Ada gazed into its face for a long moment, awed by the apparition's beauty, before she realised that she was gazing into her own face, or at least a version of her face. Ada reluctantly conceded that it was far more beautiful than she – the real Ada – actually was.

The vision laughed. "I am you Ada, everything you can be. I am the voice of your heart." Soothing music rippled in the words.

"You are a siren," Ada whispered in realisation. The music, the beautiful mist-formed body; it was all how the dragnoss guardians had described it. A real siren, sent from the dragons to help her to follow her heart.

The siren smiled in assent.

If this was a siren then what was that other apparition? Ada frowned. Iris had said that the dragons sent sirens and Yhari gave something called a synaiad. Was that *thing* a synaiad?

Ada suddenly realised that the oppressive grip on her mind had loosened. She turned to see if the other 'her' was still there, but the siren grasped her hands.

"Don't look at it. Ignore that thing with all your strength. It belongs to the parasite, trying to make you feel worthless and diseased so that you think you need it. You don't. It's telling nothing but lies. Its light is poison."

Even as the siren spoke, Ada felt the synaiad push into her mind, projecting the image of Ada's monstrous reflection in the mirrorstone again, and its message resounded in her brain: *You know this is true.*

"Ignore it," the siren pleaded. "Fill your thoughts with the things you know and love."

So the battle began.

Ada tried the siren's tactics, but she could never fully silence the synaiad's whisperings and mind-proddings. She couldn't even think about her other worries under the weight of the synaiad's conviction. Recreation also failed: if she managed to get properly absorbed in a book or activity for a minute, one stray thought would spark them off again. Not that the accusing synaiad waited for stray thoughts. It persistently and abruptly interrupted her thoughts and it was so powerful. It didn't often speak as the siren did, instead it pressed its meaning directly onto her mind, but when it pressed, it pressed *hard.* At times Ada was quite convinced that it was telling her the truth, but that was unthinkable!

She was slowly being torn in two. The days passed in agonising slowness as synaiad and siren warred. At night there was nothing to silence the conflicting voices and in the day there was no-one to distract her. She wandered restlessly backwards and forwards unable to settle to anything. Even locked away from everyone else's infuriating ways, she had no peace.

Occasionally the siren's soothing voice calmed her, but far more frequently the other *thing* dominated, weighing her down with depressive gloom.

She was going mad.

"Saupa won this battle." The siren reassured her in a rare moment of calm. "I know you have as much strength as he has – more even! Believe in yourself! You are destined to bring peace to the southern nations, just like the Oracle said. Perhaps not as you first thought and not as Saupa imagines, but you will find another way to bring peace. You just need to win this fight now. Resist! Stay in control!"

I will, I will! Ada thought, until the synaiad returned even stronger. Its mere stare made Ada shrink back. She grew afraid of catching sight of her own arms or hands, for fear the light had turned them into blackened charcoal again.

One day the synaiad stood directly in front of her, eye to eye and thundered into her mind.

You love darkness rather than light because your deeds are evil.

The sheer force of the words flattened all other thoughts or resistance. Ada cowered back, uselessly trying to block her ears, but the words were inside her head, repeating themselves getting louder and louder.

You love darkness rather than light because your deeds are evil.

I'm not a monster! I'm not evil! I love light! You're evil for doing this to me! Ada screamed back in her head.

As she said those last words, her tormentor opened up its mouth and repeated:

"*You love darkness rather than light because your deeds are evil. Everyone who does evil hates the light and will not come into the light for fear that their deeds will be exposed.*"

Only this time as it spoke, Ada saw light streaming from its mouth. That light. *His* light. Ada backed away but the light shot towards her.

She held up arms to shield herself then gazed at her hands in horror as they blackened and withered and her glass skin began to peel and flake like paper turned to ash.

Ada screamed and fell over backwards.

The chamber door crashed open.

Ada looked up at the royal official who was peering down at her in concern, two guards behind him.

She clambered to her feet, flushing self-consciously, but inwardly crying with relief. The voices and light had vanished.

"Sorry, I...I had a nightmare."

The man looked relieved if unconvinced, but he spoke briskly. "Your presence is required at the palace. Come."

24

Trial

Ada was propelled forward. The double doors behind her shut with a definite thud.

Talk buzzed like a hive of angry bees. Every cranny of the Great Hall was packed with the nobility, even the galleries were full. Most stood, some sat; all were looking at her, none too pleased. There were far too many for her to recognise, and so many strange hostile faces were overwhelming. She fixed her gaze towards the throne. King Rencival was there in full royal regalia, and to his left sat Lady Elina.

Elina's mouth gave her the slightest twitch of a reassuring smile. Ada took courage, stiffened her back, glided up the length of the hall and dropped into a full curtsey at the foot of the dais. She stayed down; eyes fixed on the floor.

The air quivered into silence.

"Lady Ada il Dura," Rencival's voice was sterner than she had ever heard it before. "You have been accused of high treason: namely, conspiring alongside your father, Lord Dura, in collusion with foreign powers to overthrow our royal person and court. How do you answer this charge?"

High treason? Ada pushed a fist into the floor, leaning into its solidity. She answered, keeping her head downcast but letting her voice ring loud for all to hear. "I am Your Majesty's loyal servant. I know nothing of such plans and would not have been part of them if I had. Furthermore, it has yet to be proved to me that my father is guilty of such a crime."

Whispers ran riot. One voice called, "Hear, hear!"

Ada's heart lifted. She was not alone.

Rencival commanded her to stand and indicated a small wooden bench for her to sit on. He addressed the room. "We heard her answer. It was well spoken as a dutiful daughter. But this is a serious accusation and must be considered properly. Lord Rothford, you may proceed."

The red-faced lord rose and jerked a bow. "The executioners are ready and await Your Majesty's command."

The rest of his words were lost on Ada. *The executioners were ready*? This was a show trial; her fate was already decided. It didn't matter if she was innocent, she was guilty by association. They were going to make a display of her death, sending a warning to all potential traitors.

Nausea clutched her throat. Her heart pounded in her ears. The room seemed far away. Sound and sight swam in distortion, as if everything were behind a wall of water.

A familiar voice drew her back to her senses. Rishard was talking. With an effort she reeled her mind back to her body. He was being questioned by Rothford, although he kept looking her way, his eyes pleading. *What was he saying*? She still had trouble focusing. There was something about Elina, an attack, her father's horse, her father's grooms...

Rishard was gone.

Two filthy men in shackles were brought forward. When Rothford asked them to confirm that they were grooms at the Dura mansion, Ada's heart sank in unhappy recognition. The grooms spoke fast, their voices high: they hadn't gone to kidnap the Lady Elina, oh no, they would never! No, they were meant to rescue her. Lord Dura had sent word by his steward, Master Kessler, that there were whispers of a plot to kidnap Lady Elina that night, and had sent them to watch one of the likely routes. If they saw her, they were to intercept and rescue her, and once liberated they should calm the lady using some poppy (Elina's face tightened grimly) and they were to take her on Lord Dura's own horse to the Old Lute tavern. They were to then send word and keep her under guard until Lord Dura arrived, and he would escort her elsewhere. But the carriage had come too fast for them to stop it before the rope and everything went wrong.

"But why did you fight Count Frénore? You must have recognised the man engaged to your master's daughter."

"We thought he was one of the kidnappers. He came out of nowhere, charging in from behind – and it was dark! We didn't see him properly until afterwards. Please masters, we were just trying to save the lady as Master Kessler instructed us."

"It seems that we need to speak to this steward," King Rencival said.

"We cannot sire. Of the two men the Nordlannders publicly arrested, one was Lord Dura's steward and the other was Lord Saupa's personal scribe – supposedly a runaway, although we can now assume that he was actually a go-between. They were placed in the royal prison. However, someone helped them escape, killing several guards and another prisoner, leaving no witnesses. Thus, Dura's steward is conveniently unavailable to give an account for himself or his master."

First her father and now Kessler were gone? The lonely stretch of the accused bench felt hard beneath Ada.

Yet it was her intervention that had caused the change of custody from the Nordish soldiers to the royal prison. If guilty, why complicate the rescue of key witnesses who could condemn her? She stored the thought away for her defending argument.

Rothford himself next told of Lord Dura and Saupa's argument at the ambassador's reception, followed by Chancellor Elkron's testimony about searching the Dura mansion, finding Ada alone in the empty dovecot and the incriminating letter in the strong room.

"And so," Rothford concluded, "with all the suspicious events that had occurred that night, Lord Dura's guilt appears ever clearer."

"Enough!" Rencival commanded. "Lord Rothford, you instigated these proceedings against Lady Ada, yet so far, your evidence has focused on her father. Do you have substantial proof against Lady Ada herself?"

Rothford's rosy face flushed to new rubicund depths. "Yes sire." He called the household chamberlain, who, after repeating the eavesdropped conversation, testified that Saupa had had a private audience with Ada.

The crowd stirred. The atmosphere hardened.

Rothford questioned her next. "Lady Ada, did Ambassador Saupa visit you?"

"Yes."

"Why?"

"To correct my ideas about Burning Hearts."

Lord Rothford blinked, taken aback by the swift ease of her answer. "Why would he do that?"

Ada raised an eyebrow. "If you recall, I did interrupt the Nordish guards imprisoning two Burning Hearts. As most of the court here witnessed, I contended that they had no right to assert Nordish law here in Aven."

Murmured agreement softened the air.

"Yes, yes. No-one disputes that," Rothford returned testily. "Although your little scene did provide the Nordlannders with a pretext to be offended and end their sham of peaceful talks."

The murmurs froze.

"But returning to your private conversation with Lord Saupa," Rothford continued. "He did not invite you to join forces with him? To commit to a loyalty higher than that owed to your king?"

In a sense that was exactly what Saupa had done, yet it was twisted out of context. *How could Rothford know that? Iris. Had they hurt her?* Ada's heart quickened.

How should she answer? She had delayed too long already; she must answer before her silence was deemed an admission of guilt. "He urged me to answer the call to obey the dragons above all else."

"Even if it meant betraying the kingdom?"

"No, we only spoke about loyalty to the dragons."

"So you agreed to join him?"

"I merely confirmed what was already true," Ada spoke slow and clear. "That I was a loyal servant to the dragons, as I trust you are, Lord."

Someone laughed. Rothford spun around, barking an order to the court officials over the rising tide of noise.

Ada sank back onto the bench, trying to hide her trembling. It *wasn't enough*. Smart answers wouldn't clear her or resolve Rothford's arguments.

Iris appeared, white-faced but apparently unharmed. Yet Ada's heart sank at the sight of her as she remembered Iris's innocent candour. Rothford would be able to twist her words easily.

Judging by Rothford's face, he was thinking the same. "You are Lady Ada's maid?"

"Yes."

"And Lord Dura instructed you to take the Nordish ambassador to Lady Ada, is that right?"

"Master chamberlain said they were Lord Dura's instructions. I did not see Lord Dura himself."

Ada's heart quickened They only had the chamberlain's word that her father had been there with Saupa.

"But you took Lord Saupa in and remained while he talked with Lady Ada?"

"Yes sir."

"Did he ask her to join his side in war?"

"He urged her to join the fight for the dragons against Yhari, yes."

"Against...who?"

Ada smiled despite herself. She had underestimated the value of Iris's truth-telling and almost pitied Rothford's bewilderment: Iris must have been more circumspect during any earlier interrogation.

"Yhari: the living light who dwells within Burning Hearts. He gives them their name and peace." Iris's voice had grown in strength.

"I object!" Chief Dragnoss Guardian Callum surged to his feet. "We are not here to listen to dragon heresy."

"Yes," Rencival agreed, although amusement belied the word. "Do keep to the matter in hand Rothford."

Tight-lipped, Rothford bowed. "As your majesty wishes." He turned a furrowed brow upon Iris. "On that same night, Lady Ada was found alone in Lord Dura's aviary. Did Lady Ada ever use the messenger birds?"

"I cannot say. I believe she visited the tower for solitude, since servants were not permitted entry there."

"Quite. Lord Dura's birds were valuable; he wanted to protect them. They were his means of communicating with his southern estates, allowing him to co-ordinate his trade – and perhaps he used them to communicate to other places, and make other arrangements. But if access to the birds was so protected, can you suggest why, on that particular evening, all Lord Dura's messenger birds went missing?"

"Missing?" Iris's shock was too genuine to be doubted.

"Yes." The blunt word held satisfaction. "And Lady Ada was discovered next to the empty cage. Which begs the question, if the birds' uses were entirely innocent, why remove them? And why should the birds disappear when Lady Ada was alone with them?"

All eyes were on Iris as she opened her mouth.

Ada clutched at the bench. Her pulse throbbed the gallows drumbeat. The truth about smuggling Orla out would sound flimsy: it would condemn not convince. At best Iris would sound like a loyal maid, trying to make up an excuse to save her mistress; at worst they would convict her too. O *Iris, what have I got you into*?

"We have heard enough."

Everyone jumped.

It was King Rencival who had spoken. He continued, his face like flint. "Dismiss the witness and summon the executioners."

"Sire!" Lord Kishere cried out. "Lady Ada hasn't had a chance to answer."

"There is no need for her to answer," the king replied. "Summon the executioners."

Ada's stomach melted through her feet. Her breath dragged in shallow spurts. A blank terror blotted everything else out. The terror took shape: the synaiad. No! Ada shrank back. She couldn't face death, not with that thing crushing her.

Feet passed in front of her.

She blinked. Three men dressed in black were kneeling before the king, presenting spiked shackles, ropes, whips and a drawn sword. In a moment they would come for her.

"Hear my judgement." Rencival's voice rang from a great distance. "The case against Lord Dura is considerable. As such all his lands and property are forfeit to the crown, until such time as Dura presents himself to answer these allegations. He must then prove his innocence or face the full penalties of the law.

"As for Lady Ada: the proofs against her comprise of her blood relations to a suspected traitor; publicly aggravating the ambassadors of a foreign power, and giving them excuse to abandon peaceful negotiations; a private interview with an enemy and her suspicious location when detained. While her father's own guilt has yet to be tried, we will not condemn her to death on such proofs. By my first decree she is already disinherited in penury. To preserve her life, she must now prove her fealty. If she fails, the executioners will be summoned again, but for now they are dismissed."

The men in black rose and bowed.

Ada swooned.

25

Departure

"I'm sorry about all the ceremony with the executioners," King Rencival said. "Any trial for high treason begins with stating that the executioners are ready and concludes by summoning them, either for their dismissal or to tell them to get to work."

Ada gulped back her drink. Get to work? She lowered her goblet, hand shaking.

They were seated face to face in the council chamber, Chancellor Elkron hovering in the background.

"It was Rothford's fault," Rencival continued. "He's pig-headed and too vocal by half. And he stirred up too much trouble to be ignored."

"Your Majesty showed that you listen and engage with the concerns of your councillors," Elkron murmured.

"My Chancellor believes I am too cavalier," Rencival said to Ada. "But I still think it would have been a better use of time to search for Dura or, better still, pursue and annihilate those Nordlannders. I can still see Prince Ellis's smug face as they drove away."

"Attacking them would have sparked retaliation. We'd have been at war within the month," Elkron said.

"Which should have delighted the Nordlannders," Rencival returned bitterly. "That's why they came here, wasn't it? To destabilise us from within, and tenderise us into a juicy morsel for when they do invade. It's inevitable. At least obliterating those two would have been a sweet pre-revenge." He fell into a moody silence.

"Your Majesty said I was to prove my fealty," Ada finally ventured. "How?"

"I'm sending you as my ambassador to Sendiva."

Ambassador? A month ago, such an appointment would have thrilled her; now she only felt tired and woefully out of her depth.

And to *Sendiva*? The name conjured up visions of snowy peaks and purple valleys; sweet-scented heather and the stink of peat; untamed gales and roaming wolves; wild heath and thick forests. These images had been forged many years ago when her tutor had spoken of his travels. As she had grown older, Ada questioned how truthful his dramatic tales had been, but everyone agreed that the mountainous kingdom on Aven's western border was a wild land of barbarians. For some strange reason, the idea of going there did not thrill her as it once did.

She didn't understand why he had chosen her. For the briefest of moments, she wished that Yhari's light would reveal Rencival's inner workings and show whether any ignoble intention darkened him, but all she could see was the very solid body of a lantyn, a lantyn who was still her king with the power of life and death over her.

She bowed her head. “What message does Your Majesty wish me to take?”

Rencival stood straight and tall. He answered with ringing authority. “You will go to King Daelan and warn him of the threat of war. We have seen the self-styled Emperor of Nordlann extend his empire and tribute territories year by year; most recently by conquering our eastern neighbour Errivel. His recent interference in our own court proves that he is beginning his next campaign. It is only a matter of time before he attempts to add both of our lands as provinces to his domain. We are the two last countries who stand independent of him on this side of the Achille Sea. It is in both of our interests that I ask for the alliance of our two nations against this northern menace.”

He paused and stepped forward, putting a hand on her shoulder and looked straight into her eyes. “I have chosen you, Ada il Dura, because I believe that you are not a traitor and you are not afraid to speak up for what you believe is right. So then, as my loyal subject, I command you to speak well for the sake of peace.”

“Forgive me sire for questioning your command, but I do not think I am the best person to act as your ambassador. I fear I would bring ridicule to your name and in my inexperience, I may unwittingly cause more enmity.”

“No other objections?” asked Rencival, the twinkle returning to his eye. “The small matter of treason of which your father is accused? You have never travelled and do not know what clothes to take with you? Supposing it rains, then what would you do? Aha! You smile at last! Even if it is the polite, insipid kind. Lady Ada, I forbid you to worry. I am sure you will prove capable."

"Thank you, but I am afraid –"

"Well you need not fear. I won't send you alone: Sir Alec Garnet will accompany and advise you. But I still need you to go, because out of all my court you were willing to be seen publicly sympathising with Burning Hearts and Sendiva is a country of Burning Hearts. You better take that maid of yours along too, and she can tell you all about their ways – yes, I know she's one of them. Now you best be going and make what preparations you must."

"Sendiva?" Iris's eyes shot wide open.

Poor girl. She has probably never even left Casida! Ada did her best to reassure Iris with tales of the country's beauty, borrowing the imagery her tutor had used. Ada found that she was unintentionally calming her own fears as she spoke, rekindling the magic of those old stories as she retold them.

Even as she spoke, the door was flung open.

Two men entered. One dumped his burden on the floor. "Your packsaddles," he said by way of explanation and departed.

Ada and Iris viewed them in dismay. "They're so small," Ada exclaimed, thinking of the fine clothes needed to appear as an ambassador. "Can't we use my box and put it in the carriage?"

"No," replied the remaining man. His voice held gruff authority. "Once we cross the border there'll be few roads suitable for carriages and we'll travel on horseback. It'll save time if you ladies pack light now."

Ada ignored the disparaging tone. "You are our escort?"

He nodded. "Sir Alec of Garnet. At you service." He added the last bit as an afterthought.

"Garnet? I'm not familiar –"

"It's near Frew. Northwest. Small place. Beneath your notice I'd expect. We'll leave at dawn. Dragons' help with your packing." He stomped out.

Sir Alec Garnet from the northwest who referenced the dragons, and would accompany her on a mission intended for peace...Perhaps the Oracle's prophecy hadn't failed: she had simply misinterpreted it. The trial had been a near miss, but she had emerged safely as the dragons had promised. Yet was she merely re-interpreting the prophecy to fit changing events?

The dragons or Yhari. She could not go on like this indefinitely. One side would have to win. If only she could go back to her comfortable certainty in the dragons, yet that would mean never having seen the true beauty of Yhari's light within Kessler and Iris. And if she were to ever enjoy that beauty for herself, she would have to confront all its associated terror: the synaiad, the relentless light penetrating her through and through and submitting to Yhari as master. On top of that, she would be cut off from the dragons forever. She shuddered at the thought of all that meant. There would be no going back. How could she ever dare to take such a step? She had lost too much already; most of what she had taken for granted was gone, while the position and fame she had achieved were hollow mockeries of her earlier ambitions. Her whole future, once so certain, was full of doubts.

"How long will we be gone, my lady?" Iris asked, as she laid out the various clothes.

Ada pushed away her pre-occupations for more practical worries. She eyed the pile, wondering how to whittle down the wardrobe. "I don't know exactly. If the roads are as rough as Sir Alec says, that will slow us down. I suppose some lightweight clothes with a heavy travel cloak will have to do for the journey, but it's tricky if I am to look the part of an ambassador when we arrive at King Daelan's court."

After a long pause, Iris said, "I was thinking about leaving Orla and being away from home, my lady."

Shamefaced, Ada asked after the child.

"She's safe with my family," Iris replied.

"You have a family?" Ada asked stupidly.

Iris nodded. "My parents, my sister Eleanor and my brother Flynn."

"Ah." Why should she be surprised that Iris had a family? "You should go to them."

Iris smiled and said she would after the packing was finished. She also insisted that Ada sit and eat something. Ada gratefully fell into an easy chair, and accepted a laden plate that Iris seemed to conjure from thin air. She sucked on a slice of fruit slowly, savouring the flavour. She could almost feel the sweet juice trickling strength back into her. Never mind her status, being alive was a joy.

Ada watched Iris work, deft and swift now she was unhindered by a sluggish-brained mistress.

Kind, faithful Iris...

Time collapsed into a hazy stream.

Ada could remember little of how she got to bed, but the next thing she knew, Iris was at her bedside rousing her. Ada dragged herself up and – oh bliss! – had a thorough wash in the warm water Iris had prepared. Once dressed, they descended to the courtyard together.

In the cool, pre-dawn light they saw a company of men with horses busy around an empty carriage. Ada quickly caught sight of Sir Alec who was directing affairs. He saw them and approached.

"Your ladyship." He jerked a bow. "I trust –"

"Ada!"

The cry shattered the air. Ada turned and saw Rishard sprinting through the gateway. He was all askew, with his jerkin slipping off a shoulder and his shirt billowing loose.

Sir Alec barked and some of his men ran forward and caught hold of Rishard. They struggled as he ploughed forward, but they eventually ground him to a halt. Above the kerfuffle Rishard bellowed, "Let me go! Let me go! *Ada!*"

Ada tried to go to him but Sir Alec grabbed her arm and held her fast. "The king did not wish for you to meet each other."

Seeing Ada being restrained drove Rishard into a frenzy. "Let go of my future wife!" he roared. A flock of birds shot up from the rooftop in alarm.

Ada had never seen him like this before: never seen him angrier; never heard him shout like that; and she'd never felt so happy to see him. Her heart sang and ached at the same time. He hadn't abandoned her after all.

Once more she stepped towards Rishard. Sir Alec began another protest but Ada looked him coolly in the eye. "We have all but met already; it would be discourteous not to greet each other now. And the king would not want his ambassadors to be uncivil." She pulled herself free and moved on.

Sir Alec followed her closely and he called for his men to step aside. Unhindered, Rishard strode forwards, but stopped abruptly at an arm's length distance. He glared at Sir Alec. "May we have some privacy?"

With obvious reluctance Sir Alec retreated a short way, but his eyes remained fixed on them.

Rishard leant forward, speaking soft and fast. "Ada, I know what I said when we last met. Forgive me. I was a fool and I can't tell you how sorry I am. I've been trying to see you but they wouldn't let me. I'm sorry about the trial and now *this* – Elkron told me. I mean, *Sendiva!* Of all places!"

Ada whispered. "I'm sorry too. But I must go: I must prove my fealty, remember?"

"Then I'm coming with you. I am betrothed to you. I at least ought to accompany you for protection."

"That is not permitted." Sir Alec had returned. "His Majesty has chosen Lady Ada to be his ambassador and me to be her escort. You, Rishard il Frénore, are commanded to stay here and prove your valour in the king's cause when needed."

Rishard went very still but there was a struggle in his eyes.

Ada stepped forward and took his hand. "Please, Rishard, don't do anything stupid. You can't get me out of this, so let me go, all the happier knowing that the king won't have anything against you."

He still stirred restlessly.

"Please Rishard. I need someone to stay here, someone I can trust to take a closer look into my father's case. Please?"

"You trust me?" His eyes glowed. "I will do everything in my power." He stepped forward and leant towards her face.

She was pulled away.

Men appeared from nowhere, pinning Rishard in at either side. He fought and yelled furiously at them, then called after Ada as Sir Alec all but dragged her to the waiting carriage.

Ada found herself unceremoniously hoisted up. Iris was bundled in after her. A whip cracked. The horses started forwards and they were whisked away.

Ada leant out of the window, trying to catch one more look, but all was dust and confusion.

The carriage jolted her down into her seat. She flopped back limply, feeling ripped in half. Her hands twisted themselves on her lap in an agony of helplessness. Iris reached over, her hands stilled Ada's, grasping them with silent comfort. Yet Ada saw that Iris's own eyes were brimming with tears and her lips could only writhe in attempts to smile. The familiar had been uprooted for her too.

Ada pulled Iris into a hug. Iris stiffened, thawed and returned the embrace.

"We will return," Ada promised. As her thoughts raced over the unresolved mysteries about her father, Kessler and Yhari, she added, "And I will find answers." Yet even as she said it doubt assailed her. *Were there any real answers? Any firm foundations?*

The veil fluttered back. Yhari reached out to her, inviting her, drawing her in, promising all the answers she needed, offering a torrential flood of love. Ada hesitated, afraid. His light might be the perfect way to either lose or find herself: one step and she could be washed away.

Epilogue

Elkron stepped up to Rencival, a blue figure among blue-grey shades. The king glowered westward as he leant against the battlements of the outer wall. Beyond them, outside the reach of the castle's shadow, rooftops flushed golden-pink with the rising sun. It would be a beautiful day.

"They have departed," Elkron reported.

Rencival grunted, swirling the goblet. "Sir Alec has no qualms about his orders?"

"None. He is a good soldier and Your Majesty's loyal servant."

They watched the silver dome of the dragnoss as it caught the dawn's dazzle.

Eventually Elkron spoke again. "She's a nice young thing. Pity."

Rencival slammed his goblet onto the battlement and spun around to Elkron. "We will do what we must for the sake of peace, as you are so fond of reminding me. You started me on this path, you will walk it with me to the bitter end!" He stalked away.

The chancellor watched him go before reaching to pick up the abandoned goblet. But the king had left it on the brink. As Elkron's fingers grazed its edge, the cup teetered and it fell.

THE GREEN EMBER
S. D. SMITH
ILLUSTRATED BY ZACH FRANZEN
THE DARK STAR
H. R. HESS
EXTRACTED
RICH CASTRO